# Trauma and Dissociation

## Understanding Early Trauma, Mind Programming and Installed Dissociative Identity Disorder

Pat Frankish and
Carrie Anne Smith

Pavilion

# Trauma and Dissociation:

## Understanding Early Trauma, Mind Programming and Installed Dissociative Identity Disorder



Published by:

Pavilion Publishing and Media Ltd
Blue Sky Offices
25 Cecil Pashley Way
Shoreham by Sea
West Sussex
BN43 5FF

Tel: 01273 434 943
Email: info@pavpub.com
Web: www.pavpub.com

Published 2022



A catalogue record for this book is available from the British Library.

ISBN: 978-1-803882-03-1

Pavilion Publishing and Media is a leading publisher of books, training materials and digital content in mental health, social care and allied fields. Pavilion and its imprints offer must-have knowledge and innovative learning solutions underpinned by sound research and professional values.

Authors: Pat Frankish and Carrie Anne Smith
With a contribution and introduction from Dr Valerie Sinason
Cover design: Tony Pitt, Pavilion Publishing and Media Ltd
Page layout and typesetting: Emma Dawe, Pavilion Publishing and Media Ltd
Printing: CMP Digital Print Solutions

## Acknowledgements

Thanks are given to all the alters in the system, all the people who provide support, and a special thanks to Kelly Calpin for her continued commitment.

# Contents

## Section 3: Therapeutic approaches



## Section 4: Conclusion

# Preface

## Pat Frankish

This book has come about after many years of working together with Carrie Anne Smith. The issues that we face in this text are not easy to confront or to accommodate. What we seek to do is to give the reader an insight into the lives of people who are forced into dissociation and, as a consequence, develop many internal identities in order to cope with life. It is intended that this book should be accessible to many and helpful to both therapists and support staff. It may also be useful to newly diagnosed people who are just beginning to understand their condition, which must be a shock to them.

This is the story of a survivor and all her inside people, and it is a real story of hope for the future. It brings together theories of attachment and early trauma, the consequences when that trauma is the outcome of organised abuse, and the approaches that are therapeutic and that can lead to a positive outcome. We include a foreword by Valerie Sinason, who is the renowned international expert in the field of dissociation, and a chapter by her which sets the scene of what Carrie Anne has survived.

Carrie Anne grew up in a 'coven' family in which biological relatives were involved in her 'training' and abuse. They are now deceased, but the organisation (i.e. the coven, her family) still exists as far as we know. At the age of 16 she managed to get away and lived for a while in a sheltered scheme for teenagers. From there until the age of 30 (chronologically) she lived a chaotic life in many flats, with numerous admissions to hospital, respite residential care, and repeated recalls to the coven where her abuse continued. Since moving to safety and finding support there has been no physical contact between her and the coven, but virtual attempts are suspected to have occurred.

I first met Carrie Anne in 2010 when I was asked to offer her/them individual therapy. This was provided but then, through an enlightened CEO of the organisation responsible for her care, she/they moved into a supported living situation with therapy. This arrangement continues and has enabled her/them to be safe and to develop to the point that they now have a job and as near an ordinary life as possible, but with 24-hour staff support for safety. Medication, sharps, keys and hot stoves still have to be monitored.

# Foreword

## Valerie Sinason

In 1989, when I was 43, I had reached a period of happiness and excitement in my work at the Tavistock Clinic, the largest NHS training and treatment centre in the UK. With the backing of colleagues, including Dr Pat Frankish, we were able to show that children and adults with an intellectual disability were not only wrongly excluded from the talking therapies but were also able to make major emotional change through accessing psychotherapy. A lifetime commitment was what we all gave to this work and each assessment and treatment added to our shared knowledge. In 2000, that same group of us formed the Institute of Psychotherapy and Disability.

However, my life changed in 1989 for another reason, too. I had been working with children and adults with an intellectual disability for ten years by then, and I had found a level of abuse that was far higher than with the general population. Pat and I and others then sadly became aware that our client group not only had to deal with the difficulties of a disability but also all the negative and trauma-loaded ways they were treated.

The life-changing moment itself came in the form of a phone call from Sweden, from Anders Svensson, a psychologist and therapist working with adults with intellectual disability, who rang for help with a case of abuse so severe he had never encountered its like before. In speaking about this awful case in Pitlochry, I was beset with letters from white middle and upper middle-class women saying they were victims of Satanist abuse[1].

As I hastened to say then, and emphasise now, people are abused by every culture and religious belief, whether mainstream or not. However, the biggest fear is engendered in these alleged victims when the supernatural is used to exert power over victims and to terrify them. We could not say if the perpetrators were real Satanists or simply using the paraphernalia to frighten their victims more, however that was the name the victims gave to it. The fact that some religions believe in a real Satan made that all the more frightening, just as abuse by a Priest, Nun, Rabbi or Mullah brings in a different religious fear.

Whilst I have now worked with victims from many religions and cults, this is the first UK book since then to focus on a context which the victims believed to be Satanist.

1 You can read our account in *Treating Survivors of Satanist Abuse*, published by Routledge in 1994.

This book is to be read very slowly and carefully with the reader taking time. Despite knowing that one in four adults get abused over a lifetime, many citizens and professionals do not think about that directly; what it really means. Thinking about dissociative disorders is even harder. There are very few professional books on the subject even though multiple personality, as it used to be called, is in every international psychiatric classification.

What does it mean when the word 'I' means several? When there is no autonomy of selfhood? When you can get dressed to go and visit a friend only to find yourself asleep in a house you do not recognise? Dissociative Identity Disorder (DID) is a tragic result of trauma. It allows the child to not know how vulnerable they are because another state of mind bears the terrible memory. "Thank heavens I had DID", said Sue, aged 40. "I would never have managed an education if I had known what my parents were doing to me."

DID is the creative, brilliant defence of dividing and separating memory and thinking functions so that living can be managed as well as possible. Sue could go happily to school unaware that her alcoholic father had abused her in the night and her depressed mother hated her. She could do this because Sienna, one of her alters, took the abuse and Sarah, another alter, saw her depressed mother as a suffering saint who must be treated as precious.

But, even in the midst of this human ingenuity to hibernate in the mind, there is a further step into the abyss: 'installed DID', thought control, mind control, brainwashing. This is where the multiplicity of alters is deliberately created by the abusers to hide the secrets.

Abuse, group abuse, dissociation, installed dissociation… there are lots of hurdles to get to this. Pat Frankish, of course, got to it. And in reaching it she provided protection and offered understanding and containing and respect. This book is written alongside many survivors (in one body). They have all made sure of their safety and spent months considering the dangers of writing this book.

Many books on mind control have a false happy ending. This book does not, but nevertheless there is hope. There is admission of the scars made on mind, body and soul when going through experiences like this. Alters/personalities of the age they have been told they are, perceive their world according to that age. Those who have witnessed what is done to babies in the most abusive cults feel they know their own babyhood. Those who are told of the powers that some inside states have, believe that. Life and change is an ongoing process. Pat and Carrie Anne have not gone through altering what child states have said. They have given them the proper dignity of their own narrative. However, the reader needs to understand that, as with any biography, this does not come with forensic evidence. It comes with the emotional experience of a lived hell.

I would like to offer my congratulations to the co-editors and authors of this book for their courage in writing, and to you, reader, who reads it. And if we consider that the reader deserves praise for having the courage to read this book, think what it feels like to be the person who has actually lived some of these experiences...

# Section 1: Setting the scene

This section introduces the links between attachment, trauma and dissociation, as well as offering an overview of mind programming, the origins of mind programming techniques and its link with installed Dissociation Identity Disorder.

There are terms used throughout this book that would benefit from some description.

**Dissociative Identity Disorder (DID)** is a condition that involves several (or more) personalities living in the same body. It is a trauma response condition. Some people know they have alters and others do not. They are referred to as co-conscious or not co-conscious. **Alters** is the name given to the other personalities. Sometimes they are called 'inside people'. There is usually a **host personality** who manages day-to-day life, and the host can change over time.

The terms **cult** or **coven** are used to name the organisations that are involved in ritual abuse, which is the usual form of trauma that DID people have experienced. This usually involves being born into a ritual family, but not always. The organised abusers find vulnerable people to join them. But people with DID will have been abused from early childhood.

Some of these organisations use **mind programming** as well. This involves hypnotism and setting triggers to provoke certain types of behaviour. The person who has been mind programmed is not aware of what happens when an alter is triggered to carry out certain behaviours. A common example is to provide sexual services. Others can be to partake in rituals.

# Chapter 1: Attachment and early trauma

## Pat Frankish

Throughout this text we will be considering the impact of early trauma. Sadly, for many years, the various professions and authorities who come into contact with victims of early trauma have not been able to acknowledge this impact. This seems to partly stem from a belief that things that happen before substantial cognitive development do not have an impact on the developing child, which may also relate to theorists such as Sigmund Freud who indicated that we do not need to consider things that happened before the age of seven. This acceptance of 'non-personhood' in the first seven years of a child's life has significantly handicapped recognition of early trauma for a long time. We now know from considerable research in the last 50 years that this concept is completely incorrect and may have developed because of the difficulty of approaching very small children who cannot answer the question "what is happening to you?". Another factor is the impact of trauma on cognitive development, which may be noticed, but then assumed to be a cognitive disability. We now know that babies can be traumatised at or close to birth and at any time afterwards. We also acknowledge that the key protective factor is a secure and reliable attachment figure who is present and reliable at all times.

Donald Winnicott, John Bowlby and Margaret Mahler – all researchers working in the 1970s – provided us with very rich information about attachment, its significance, and the consequences of inadequate or failed attachment. What we will be looking at here is the extreme end of failed attachment, where the attachment process is deliberately undermined and used to establish power over the individual, so that they will obey instructions, but be dissociated from the process. The impact of the theories of these three researchers is discussed in more depth in section 3, which focuses on the therapeutic approaches to understanding and dealing with early trauma. This book is an attempt to bring the different bodies of knowledge together in a helpful way. If we consider that dissociation is the splitting of the self, we can begin to understand why there is difficulty in bringing the theories together. It is hoped that, by the end, readers will have a clearer and connected view of the issues of trauma, mind control, attachment and dissociation.

There are lots of reasons for failed attachment. The most common one, clearly, is the absence of the primary carer, which may happen if there is a serious problem at birth that prevents mother and child proceeding with their life together. There is a substantial body of information and research now that links the quality of early relationships to the positive mental health of the child and later the adult. Sue Gerhardt's book *Why love matters: How Affection Shapes a Baby's Brain* (2004) provides a good explanation of the processes involved and the outcomes. Sadly, there are often big issues of chance, circumstance and opportunity that lead to attachment difficulties and, as stated, the focus of this book is on the extreme end of attachment difficulties.

We accept that early trauma interferes with the development of healthy attachments, and one can see that the impact of weak or no attachment ability impacts on every aspect of life. Anyone interacting with someone who has never had healthy attachment will repeatedly trip up in their social interchange. If you reflect on your own experience of crossed communication with people you have met there will have been times when you have suddenly felt judged, a failure, attacked, lost, or just confused by a communication with another person that's gone wrong. And so often this is because of a confused and damaged attachment pattern. So, for example, you make a new friend and plan an outing, then at the last minute you have to make some changes. You are then met with extreme anger and verbal abuse which you do not understand. Then you ask the question, "why does this person react so angrily to being let down?", and you can surmise that they have been let down by attachment figures in their early childhood and are left with an inability to accept or adjust to changing expectations.

As we go through this book you will appreciate that, when talking about extremes of attachment failure, together with a deliberate attacking of the attachment process, we are talking about activities that are used in order to gain control of the individual. This process leads to disassociation deliberately created in order to maintain that control. There is a difference between weak or poor attachment behaviour from adults on the one hand, and deliberate manipulation of the relationship to produce installed alters on the other. Many people have had a poor experience of parenting. Fortunately, few people experience the extremes of deliberate ritual abuse, but those who do are seriously harmed and in need of understanding and help.

It is extremely difficult to accept that adults, particularly parents, can actively disturb the development of attachment in the child. However, that is what we know happens when there is organised abuse. The words 'cult' or 'coven' are often used for these organisations, and these words do tend to evoke images of witches and pointy hats and suchlike. There is no doubt that some organisations involved in ritual abuse that do have the paraphernalia, costumes, ritual fires and events and suchlike. They are, naturally, very secretive organisations and the people who manage to escape them are usually not believed. Consequently, they drift into mental health services, are treated as seriously mentally ill, or they proceed to take their own lives. If they attempt to tell the police about what is happening to them, they may disappear. In one of the later chapters in the lived experience section there is a story of an alter who was expected to take on the role of an abuser. This was shortly before the host alter at that time was able to escape from the abusive situation they were in. This clearly took an enormous amount of courage; courage which has led to the ability and willingness to write this book.

## References

Sue Gerhardt (2004) *Why Love Matters: How affection shapes a baby's brain*. London: Routledge.

# Chapter 2: Dissociation and mind programming

Pat Frankish

This chapter expands on the last to look specifically at mind programming, which is a form of mind control. What is mind programming? And who uses it? The old-fashioned term 'brain washing' tends to be associated with spies and conspiracies. George Orwell's book *1984* (1949) described a process of mass mind control that reduced a whole population to semi-automatons, obeying the rule of those in charge. Throughout human history there have been people, organisations and governments who have used mind control to control behaviour. Hitler (*Mein Kampf*, 1925) experimented, using doctors and torture techniques, to see if he could make people do what he wanted without question. And we know that, to some extent, he succeeded. So, what are the factors that drive some people to exercise mind programming? And what are the techniques that are employed? And what is their impact on the victims?

The answer to why anyone or any group of people would choose to use mind programming is, of course, power. Humans have a real problem with feeling powerless, and those who seek to be powerful have perhaps experienced feeling powerless to such an extent that it was intolerable, leading them to exert power over others to minimise their intolerable feelings. If such individuals then find a group of similar individuals, they can become convinced that what they are doing is right and acceptable. They feed off each other. They may be drawn to each other. But the source of the problem is their own early experience, which will have been of cruel parenting. Little babies are omnipotent. They believe that the world is theirs and revolves around them. If they are gently coaxed over the first three or four years of life into a realisation that this is not so, they will grow up with a meaningful relationship with power and power issues. If they are overwhelmed and treated as less than others, powerless to influence their life, they will grow up either so damaged that they cannot function, or with a determination to never feel like that again, and will seek to exert power over others. This provides the environment for the ritual abuser. Some will be given a diagnosis of psychopathic personality disorder and may be locked away for the safety of others. Some will find like-minded people and form a group, or cult, to further their sadistic desires.

Mind programming is used in abusive cults to make members comply with activities relating to their rituals. There will be many references to rituals and how they work, what they do. The victims of mind programming react in different ways. Inevitably some go on to become perpetrators, advancing up the hierarchy to become mind programmers themselves. Some die as part of ritual sacrifices, some take their own lives, some become so damaged mentally that they become long-term mental health patients. And some, the people who are contributing to this book, become dissociated. They have a condition called Dissociative Identity Disorder (DID) recognised as a post-traumatic stress disorder, and this is a survival response to the experience of being mind controlled.

The next question to consider is this: when might these cults develop and flourish? The answer is mixed, they tend to flourish during periods of history when there is a high number of vulnerable young people. In times of austerity and where there is a lack of state protection for vulnerable people, there will be an increased likelihood of growing power imbalances. This type of environment is not country- or race-specific. It can be anywhere where there are serious imbalances in power structures.

Let's consider a child born into a cult family. Some of them will be sacrificed. Others will not arrive at the right time to be sacrificed so will need to be looked after or primed to become future adult members of the cult. And the priming is via mind control. The first task of the parents in this situation is to make sure that the child never tells anyone else what is going on. This means that there is a primary need for the child to have a personality and presentation that they take into the ordinary world of nursery, school or other environments and activities, and which they present to their friends and other children. In addition, they need a personality and presentation that will engage with the Satanist rituals.

So at least two alternative selves are required from the beginning. What seems to happen is that the treatment of the child in the early years is designed to prevent the development of a secure sense of self, and this remains a significant difficulty for the rest of the victim's life. In an ideal world, a child develops from the isolated emotional state of the new-born to the established personality of the 3½ to 4-year-old child (Mahler, 1979). When this progression is prevented, the insecure, split-off parts of the self can easily be manipulated by those in positions of power. It is likely that the main technique used is to disturb the early feeding regime, with multiple feeders preventing the development of secure attachment to any one person, and perhaps food given that has narcotic or other substances added. Having been prevented from establishing a secure attachment, the child becomes susceptible to further training, constantly seeking security and being easily led to believe that security is on offer. The user can then train the insecure split off parts to carry out certain behaviours in response to triggers. These triggers can be anything, but in formal training it will usually be a song or a phrase, may be a colour or an article. For example, the split off part could be trained to self-harm when they hear a certain tune. Or they may be trained to overeat, undereat, vomit, or show other food disturbances in response to an odour, a word or, again, a tune.

A child who has been trained to behave in certain ways when triggered by certain things will be significantly disadvantaged in the ordinary world, and will often be seen as someone suffering from severe mental illness. And within the cult or coven that they grow up in, they will be obedient and perform anything that is asked of them. Sadly, this is often very negative, including extremes of sexual and violent behaviour. The common themes that have emerged in therapy sessions and reported by Valerie Sinason, Alison Miller and others working in this field, are of young girls and women being impregnated during rituals, and then for their babies to be sacrificed in further rituals. Clearly this is not something that young girls would consciously agree to. Sometimes they do not remember that it happened, as it was an alternative self that was involved. Then, during therapy, this alternative self can bring it back into consciousness with obvious distress. But at the time of carrying out the activities they are completely under the control of their abusers. They have become so mind-controlled that they are not able to protest, or even to know what is happening to them.

All of this raises questions as to the role of parents and whether they are complicit in what happens to their children, or if they are also mind controlled and programmed to behave in the way they do. It does seem that victims of mind programming are usually very competent at keeping the authorities in the dark, especially those with DID because they themselves, or parts of themselves, are kept in the dark by the presence of their alters. This goes back to the establishment of a self that is able to engage with ordinary life. The child who goes to school every day, looks normal, behaves normally and does the schoolwork as expected, is not going to arouse any suspicion. The child themselves does not know what is going on in the other part of their life, as there is an unconscious boundary within the psyche that prevents them from knowing. This is true dissociation. Professionals who are aware of this condition may detect it in children that they meet, but they will rarely be able to prove it. This is because the parents will be very consistent in what they say, and the child will support them from that part of the self that has been trained to do so.

One of the things that has been noticed in working therapeutically with people who have endured mind programming, is that their natural psychological defence mechanisms have sometimes produced non-programmed dissociations. Dissociation as a condition does occur separately from mind programming, as a response to trauma, and can be seen in any child or adult who has experienced trauma in their developmental stages of life. As the experience of rituals will be terrifying at times, it is not surprising that this is experienced as traumatic and that natural dissociations occur. It adds to the complexity of the individual system and to the individuality. Some mind-programmed people are the same, some of the alters have occurred naturally through traumatic disassociation, and some of them have been trained through mind control programming. Some people with mind control programming remain co-conscious and are aware of other selves. But some are not aware at all and are often surprised to be told, if they ever receive the help they need, that they have done something of which they have no recall. Most people have some child selves inside and this can, of course, make it dangerous to drive a vehicle or engage in other adult pursuits. Switching to a child self while driving a car can be terrifying and has been reported elsewhere.

## Therapy and responses

Therapeutic work with this population therefore becomes very complex, but if the model can be understood and tolerated by the person undergoing therapy, they have an opportunity to process some of the trauma and despair and progress to a way of living that is tolerable. One of the very distressing aspects for them, however, is that they cannot usually stop the mind control programming, only learn to recognise what triggers it, and how to manage the consequences of it being triggered. Many of them will need 24-hour support, and for someone else to be alert to activated programming. It is sadly the case that most of the programming is destructive and would potentially lead to severe injury, a return to the abusers, or death.

Most people with complex mind programming who have had an opportunity to consider what has happened to them, will arrive at an understanding of the psyche as a system, with multiple parts, on multiple levels. They will learn that there will usually be a host alter who may change from time to time, and that there will be others who have clear and specific roles within the system. There will be others who are very fragile and susceptible to having programmed behaviours activated. One of the consequences of mind control programming is an insecurity about everything. Trust has been eroded at the beginning of life, and this has happened deliberately to prevent the establishment of a secure self. Consequently, everyone is viewed with suspicion and even if a therapeutic relationship is established with one alter, it does not necessarily spread to others, and the relationship remains insecure and unreliable. When the alters can work together things can get better, but this can take years of therapeutic work and trustworthy support to become established.

Very few therapists have been trained to work with such complex psychological conditions as DID. The number is growing however, and, inevitably, knowledge and skill is increasing. It is hard to imagine what it is like to discover that you have other personalities inside your head. And yet at the same time it must be a relief for some people to know why they have huge gaps in their memory.

The role of therapists and support staff is often to concentrate on safety issues. In the first instance there is pressure to enable the individual to leave their family or organisation that is still abusing them. Some therapists will not engage with them until they have left, but in the writer's experience sometimes they need therapeutic support in order to be able to make the break. It goes back to attachment and trust. If a child or young person has never known anything or anyone else, they are going to be suspicious of anything that is offered. Sometimes when young children are taken into care and offered for adoption, they are very suspicious of potential adoptive parents. Sometimes this needs to be seen as a warning that the abuse in the family of origin may have included mind control programming. Of course, there will be some children who have had horrific experiences during their developmental period without the active negative influence of mind programming. But if the signs are there, the question needs to be asked. One of the indicators seems to be that a child appears to be a completely different person from time to time.

These themes are developed further by Valerie Sinason in the next chapter.

## References

Orwell G (1949) *Nineteen Eighty-Four.* London: Secker and Warburg.

Hitler A (1925) *Mein Kampf.*

Crowley A (1909) *The Book of the Law.*

Mahler M, Pine F and Bergman A (1979) *The Psychological Birth of the Human Infant.* New York: Basic.

Noble K (2011) *All of Me.* London: Piatkus.

# Chapter 3: The origins of dissociation, organised ritual abuse and installed Dissociation Identity Disorder

Valerie Sinason

While Dissociative Identity Disorder (DID), the relatively new term for Multiple Personality Disorder, is included in international classifications and there has been an increase in books, papers, television, film and documentaries about it, it remains a subject that brings unease and, as a result of that, a significant lack of professional training. Indeed, as we have found in the study of intellectual disability (formerly known as learning disability, retardation, backwardness), subjects that come under pressure to change their names are often subjects that provoke fear. In the West, the high value placed on individuality and self-hood makes the idea of multiple self-states all the more threatening.

In the Diagnostic Statistical Manual (DSM)-V (American Psychiatric Association, 2013) DID is described as a disruption of identity characterised by two or more distinct personality states or an experience of possession. The earlier understanding of Pierre Janet's idea that dissociation is impacted by trauma is transformed into a more factual definition of functioning. It is, however, the traumatic links of this condition that add to the fear of noticing, diagnosing and treating the condition, because the survivor, or the professional supporting the survivor, is all-too-often seen as the bringer of bad news who must be ignored or discredited.

In the four decades of being involved with this subject (Sinason, 2002; 2020) our field has been heartened by the number of courageous survivors and their supporters (Noble, 2011; Hoffman, 2014; Miller, 2012; Bowlby, 2014; Frankish, 2017) who have written or spoken about living with this condition. Each narrative shines a new light and brings hope to those still suffering in silence. However, national and international access to experienced mental health professionals and police officers remains inadequate.

I mention police officers in this context because, above all other mental health conditions, DID is a forensic issue. Whilst it is understood that trauma, and especially sexual abuse, can be hidden secretly in the aetiology of many mental health conditions, DID is, par excellence, a condition that comes as a result of a crime against a child, whether intentional or unintentional. DID is now seen largely as the result of two major issues joining together – abuse at an early age from an attachment figure and a disorganised attachment. As early as 1986 Putnam found that 97 out of 100 patients diagnosed with DID had experienced major early trauma with almost half having witnessed a violent death. Fonagy and Target (1995) in a survey of the literature of the time report that 90% of patients meeting DSM criteria for a dissociative disorder reported histories of childhood abuse and noted that in another study, 17 out of 20 patients had their abuse histories independently corroborated.

Dr John Bowlby (1907-90) was the giant we have to thank for attachment theory, together with the researchers whose work was made possible because of him. While just over half our population is considered to have a secure attachment, which makes for healthy reflective adulthood, almost the rest of the population are less lucky with an insecure attachment, however they can still be loved and loving. A small percentage, however, are unlucky enough to have a disorganised attachment. A disorganised attachment is where a child has the misfortune to be brought up by an attachment figure who is either frightened or frightening so there is no secure first experience to lay down foundations of self-esteem, confidence and a sense of safety. The child then has to struggle to fit themselves around the disturbed behaviours of their carer. This earliest loss of security and safety makes the child more vulnerable to abuse. The normal bodily defences of fight, flight and freeze is often not possible for a small child, especially when it is an attachment figure who is causing the pain. Amnesia between different states of mind therefore protects the child from the knowledge that they have no safe place, but it becomes a defence that brings its own problems.

Angela, for example, was eight years old and her mother had never bonded with her. A victim of child abuse herself, Angela's mother suffered from postnatal depression at the sight of her infant daughter and could not bear being with her. It was not that she hated Angela, it was that she hated herself. Angela looked just like she had as a baby and that added to how unbearable she found looking at her daughter. Without police, social services or counseling help for her own past abuse, Angela's mother's self-hate was so huge it could not be kept in her own body, despite drinking and cutting herself. The generational poison therefore poured into baby Angela, who was made to be her toxic container. Baby Angela received no loving cuddles, no affirmation of her identity.

Angela's father was an alcoholic with his own history of unworked through pain. When sober he behaved lovingly to his baby daughter. But his drug and alcohol abuse led him to sexually abuse her. In order to survive this tragic home life Angela brilliantly and spontaneously created twin protectors, a teenage boy and girl. When father abused Angela, one of the twins would appear and Angela would remain amnesic to the memory. It was only when Angela's father ran off and the twin alters, personalities or self-states were no longer needed to keep the secret that Angela's nightmares and bedwetting alerted her school to making a referral for her. Sadly (Sinason & Marks, 2021), while there has been a slow but steady increase in adults daring to refer themselves, there is a huge gap in child professionals picking up this subject given the serious lack of training. In therapy, Angela slowly developed a sense of trust and self-regulation from which she gradually became aware that her nightmares were the result of a reality her body had experienced. The twins, Adam and Annie, were helped to support Angela from the inside by joining with her. In this specific treatment the outcome was 'multigration', a term used to describe where the alters merge to become one. There are, however, many treatments where different self states knowing about each other's existence is the most realistic and successful outcome.

Work with children with DID has a good possibility of success (Renee Marks, 2021) as long as the child is in a safe home and receives proper specialist treatment. If it was their parents who were the abusers, children with DID are only safe enough to show their condition when they are in foster homes. For most, the condition continues into adulthood as they have received inadequate treatment or they have never had a safe person to speak with. After all, the fear of different states of mind linking up is akin to a phobia, given that linking up could reproduce the terror of the memories which caused the need to remain compartmentalised in the first place (van der Hart, Nijenhuis & Solomons, 2010).

Brenda was a part-time teacher in a secondary school. She loved her job and was liked and respected by the staff and pupils. She was 32 and had been a teacher for ten years. She was single and liked it that way. She worked two and a half days a week and said she devoted the rest of the time to hobbies, although she never said what they were. One day, the head teacher said a deputy headship was coming up and he would like her to apply for it. Brenda felt enormous terror before a sense of pleasure and gratitude appeared. When she got home, the pleasure disappeared and the terror increased. Words in lipstick started appearing on her mirror: "You are a thick bitch and can't teach anyone". Voices in her head began to taunt her and her GP referred her to psychiatry and a section ensued. Whilst most of the psychiatric team considered her to be schizophrenic, a new consultant with more up-to-date experience, considered the possibility of DID. In treatment it slowly emerged that the whole system of Brenda and her alters could only remain stable if there was no pressure from Wednesday to Sunday so that her 'others' had their own time. Going beyond two and a half days a week was too much for them to continue the way they were. As Sachs (2017) has pointed out, there is a significant difference between stable or unstable DID. Sexual abuse, it was discovered, had stopped once she left home to go to college but Brenda had needed to be amnesic over the extent of it.

It is a more difficult experience to realise you have DID when you are an adult, and especially if the abuse is still continuing. In my own experience, the two most common causes of DID in those over 40 are ongoing sexual abuse by family and ongoing abuse in various forms by both family and others. Additionally, for those of us who have been in the field a long time, it is clear that there are two other factors at play. Just as disorganised attachment and trauma join together to create DID, the most severe form of DID comes as a result of ritual abuse or mind programming. Together, these come under a new umbrella called installed DID.

Organised ritual abuse is a regular feature in the narrative of patients coming for DID treatment. All abuse that is linked to religious, spiritual or pseudo-spiritual/religious beliefs evokes extra fear in victims. A working definition of ritual abuse (Sinason & Aduale, 2008) is when a child or adult is made to feel that they, their families, or those they love, are doomed in this life and in an afterlife if they do not obey what they are asked to say or do. These circumstances result in a larger number of alters and more difficulties in treatment, appearing to come from an installed dissociation. There is still the disorganised attachment and early abuse but there is also deliberate torture aimed at creating different self-states – in other words, brainwashing or mind programming.

To understand the origins of mind programming, we need to consider the use of torture in every period of human history. During the decades following the Second World War, interest grew in how psychology could be weaponised and how military and intelligence personnel could be equipped with the capacity to withstand torture. 'Brainwashing' as a term was first used in English in 1950 by Edward Hunter who wanted to understand and then explain, as did the American military, how and why during the Korean war some American prisoners of war cooperated with their captors or defected to their side. An understanding of how trauma-bonding works in the family, let alone in cults, was not available then.

Research and experimentation in this area was also helped by the many experimenters who had worked for the Nazi regime  whose torture techniques were studied and built upon. Operation Paperclip, for example (Ross, 2006) brought many such Nazis into America to aid military intelligence. There was also a strong desire to know how the Chinese government appeared to make people cooperate. Operation Bluebird was approved by CIA Director Allen Dulles in 1950 and actioned in 1951 to install DID. It was later renamed Operation Artichoke and involved research on how to produce amnesia in operatives who were no longer reliable.

Project MK-Ultra[1] began in 1953 when CIA director Allen Dulles authorised experiments involving drugs, electric shock and sleep deprivation to see

1 MK came from Josef Mengele's use of the term 'Mind Kontrol'.

how behaviour was affected. MK-Ultra was brought to light by various commissions in the 1970s, including the Rockefeller Commission of 1975 and the 1977 Senate hearings, which revealed the experiments tested drugs (like LSD), sensory deprivation, hypnotism and electric shocks on a huge range of people including prostitutes, recovering drug addicts and prisoners – often without their consent. Despite MK-Ultra violating ethical norms for human experiments, the legacy of brainwashing experiments continued in US policy as we saw in Abu Ghraib, Iraq, and Guantanamo Bay.

In 1953 the brilliant psychiatrist Robert Jay Lifton, who worked with the veterans and later studied doctors who aided Nazi war crimes, interviewed former POWs as well as students and others who had been in prison in China (1954;1986;1973). By 1980 the American Psychiatric Association included brainwashing ' in the DSM-III.

Robert Jay Lifton listed eight criteria for thought reform that impact equally on all forms of mind programming and installed DID. They included milieu control, mystical manipulation, demand for purity, the cult of confession, the sacred science, loading the language, doctrine over person and dispensing of existence. This list is as painfully helpful and relevant to the environment of ritually abused people with DID as to American soldiers trapped in the Korean prison camps.

Within those working with the effects of MK-Ultra, there has also been a concerning minority narrative who spoke of Monarch Programming under an Illuminati umbrella. Clients who allege abuse from groups using the terms 'Illuminati' and 'Monarch' present with large numbers of installed dissociative parts. Rather than names, many of these alters have titles denoting their functions.

**ALPHA.** Regarded as "general" or regular programming within the base control personality; accomplished through deliberately subdividing the victim's personality.

**BETA.** Referred to as "sexual" or "sex kitten" programming, training is provided from the earliest age to become accomplished in all forms of sexuality. The greatest joy is to successfully arouse another.

**GAMMA.** Another form of system protection is through "deception" programming, which elicits misinformation, disinformation, and misdirection. This level causes problems with police evidence, discrediting the "main" person as a viable witness.

**DELTA.** This is the key part of Manchurian candidate research. The Delta is a programmed assassin developed for elite forces. Subjects are devoid of fear; very systematic in carrying out their assignment. Self-destruct or suicide instructions are layered in at this level.

**THETA** means "psychic" programming. This is a development of training that was automatic in multi-generational Satanist families anxious to show the genetic benefits of the bloodline. It is the true story behind the censored story of the men who stare at goats.

**OMEGA.** A "self-destruct" suicide form of programming. This programme is generally activated when the victim/survivor begins therapy or interrogation and too much memory is being recovered.

In the beginning of any cutting-edge subject, when it first breaks through professional fear and amnesia, we have the voice of the subject reached through the voice of the therapist or mental health professional. The child victim of domestic abuse is terrified to speak and the victim of abuse which cause DID is even more terrified. By speaking, the professional lends their voice in support. The turning point is when we witness the partnership between the survivor and their support team. This book is the result of such a combination. In writing about the extremes of DID and how it is created, we are hoping that whoever is privileged to hear from a survivor who has gone through such unbearable events will have their shock cushioned so that their heart and mind are there to help.

Jose Delgado (1974) who was based in Yale and died in 2011 could say "Man does not have the right to develop his own mind. One day armies and generals will be controlled by electrical stimulation of the brain". Against that we have the growth of attachment-based relational work. Mind programming can damage and harm children and adults, but it cannot be totally successful because there is still something unique and precious in each human that can be held onto until it is safe enough to emerge. There is more about the lived experience as you read on.

Alison Miller (2012), Wendy Hoffman (2013), Cisco Wheeler & Fritz Springmeier and Ellen Lacter have written extensively on this.

## References

Miller A (2012) *Healing the unimaginable: Treating ritual abuse and mind control.* London: Karnac.

American Psychiatric Association (2013) *Diagnostic and statistical manual of mental disorders*. (5th edition).

Bowlby X (ed) (2014) *Living with the Reality of Dissociative Identity Disorder: Campaigning Voices*. London: Karnac.

Delgado J (1974) Congressional record, No 262E Vol.118.

Epstein OB, Schwartz J & Wingfield Schwartz R (2011) (eds) *Ritual Abuse and Mind Control: The manipulation of attachment needs*. London: Karnac.

Fonagy P & Target M (1995) 'Dissociation and Trauma'. *Current Opinion in Psychiatry 8.*

Frankish P & Sinason V (2017) *Holistic therapy for people with dissociative disorders. London:* Routledge.

Hoffman W (2013) *The Enslaved Queen: A memoir about electricity and mind control.* London: Aeon Books.

Lacter E (2022) https:/endritualabuse.org

Lifton R (1954) Home by ship; reaction patterns of American Prisoners of war repatriated from North Korea. *American Journal of Psychiatry* **110** (10) 732-739.

Lifton RJ (1986) *The Nazi Doctors: medical killing and the psychology of genocide.* New York: Basic Books.

Lifton RJ (1973) *Home from the War: Vietnam Veterans – Neither Victims nor Executioners.* New York: Simon & Schuster, Touchstone Books, 1973. Reissued by Basic Books, 1985; Beacon Press, 1992; as *Home from the War: Learning from Vietnam Veterans*. New York: Other Press, 2005.

Marks J (1959) *The Search for the Manchurian Candidate*. Michigan: Times Books

Miller A (2012) *Healing the Unimaginable: Treating ritual abuse and mind control.* London: Karnac.

Noble K (2011) *All of Me*. London: Piatkus.

Putnam EW et al (1986) The clinical phenomenology of multiple personality disorder:Review of 100 recent cases. *Journal of Clinical Psychiatry* **47** 285-93.

Ross C (2006) The CIA Doctors;Human Rights Violatiojns by American Psychiatrists. Richardson: Manitou Communications.

Sachs A (2017) Through the lens of attachment relationship: stable DID, active DID and other trauma-based mental disorders. *J Trauma Dissociation* May-Jun 2017 **18** (3) 319-339.

Sinason V (2002) (ed) Attachment, Trauma and Multiplicity: Working with Dissociative Identity Disorder. London: Routledge.

Sinason V & Aduale A (2008) Talk at Safeguarding London Children quoted in Sinason V (2020) *The Truth about Trauma and Dissociation, Everything you didn't want to know and were afraid to ask.* London: Confer Books.

Sinason V & Marks PR (2021) *Treating children with dissociative disorders; attachment, trauma, theory and practice*. London: Routledge

van der Hart O, Nijenhuis ERS, Solomon R. (2010) Dissociation of the Personality in complex trauma-related disorders and EMDR Theoretical considerations. *Journal of EMDR Practice and Research* **4** (2).

van der Merwe & Sinason V (2018) *Shattered but Unbroken: Voices of Triumph and Testimony*. London: Routledge.

# Section 2: The lived experience

This section is written by Carrie Anne Smith and her alters. Some chapters are written by Carrie Anne as the host of the Dissociative Identity Disorder (DID) system, one is written by an alter 'Alistair / Protector' and some chapters include excerpts of experiences by other alters. Some of the experiences are painful and distressing.

The last two chapters in this section include details about Carrie Anne's therapy, what has worked on the journey to recovery and issues that they have faced.

Below is an introduction from the DID system of Carrie Anne. This poem reflects the lived experience of the survivors who have contributed to this book.

Please stop and gaze
on the programmers' maze
It changes with time
and is designed to amaze
you toss and you turn
but you will ever yearn
how much complexity
does the programmers learn.

I see you confused
By the programmers' muse
but he twists and he turns
in circles amused
you don't understand
just how underhand
nemesis is
when you upon it land.

Nemesis is the programmer's dream
twisting and turning you never will glean
the long winding road with dangers ahead
a brain and a spinal cord transplanted with dread
Just like the Borg based from star treks TV
The Borg queen the controller trying to control we
By placing herself in our body and mind
Who knows what she will try and will find.

The Borg queen acts in internal ESP
Communicates inside and talks outside through one free
Carrie-Anne in danger of being her mic
With the mind controller's mind she does try to strike
To her other alters are nothing but drones
She doesn't need darks and she doesn't need clones
She tries and she tries to fill you with dread
Until you are sure you'd be better off dead.

She tries to control expecting the drain
More and more knackered til you give in again
Like a crab inside a whelk shell
She flexes her claws in a way you know well
To fight without being drones is now the cause
To come together with mighty applause
To hold Carrie-Anne's arms up like Moses with the sea
To walk through the middle in a bid to be free.

Anon and Margot

# Chapter 4: Mind control methods: an understanding of what happened to us

Carrie Anne Smith

We are the system of the Dancing Dolphins. As a system, it is hard to comprehend why we were subject to experimental mind control, and yet we know of many methods that were used to manipulate our mind. To the reader, this may seem like a contradiction of terms, a system knowing about its own mind control, except for the fact that a minority of us were used in training to become people who mind controlled others ourselves. For this we are not proud and are most contrite about it, but, at the same time, it has put us in a unique position to tell of methods that we were taught about, to assist the coven in mind controlling others. It is with this in mind that we share our own experiences, to show others just how intelligent the programming community actually are when it comes to manipulating the minds of innocent Dissociative Identity Disorder (DID) systems like ours.

For our system, experimental mind control methods started at the age of just a few hours old. Witnesses to this told us that we were held upside down at a coven gathering for our birth, with our biological mother threatening to drop us on our head and kill us, which laid the foundations of trauma and terror which were to come in our early years. From the perspective of another relative, abusive behaviours such as this were regular phenomena and came under the guise of behaviourism. When Watson and Rayner (1920) were studying the psychological perspective of behaviourism, they performed a study on a boy named 'Little Albert'. This child was encouraged to play with a white rat, and treated it as a pet. After some time of the boy interacting with the rat, Watson and Rayner introduced a loud bang every time Little Albert touched it, which distressed him greatly, and this continued until he did not want to touch the animal anymore. Named classical conditioning, these kinds of conditions and actions were used on us, and we have seen and heard of other systems who have experienced them too, with many negative effects.

For systems such as ours, it is possible to see how the principles of behaviourism were used in our mind control. Within covens there are very often a number of members of the 'coven family' (as opposed to the biological family) including various coven mothers and fathers, who all exist to perform very specific tasks. Coven mothers, for example, may be very loving or abusive, which are total polar opposites to each other, and are very dangerous for little children within a DID system. A very young child may be given a very loving mother to play with, who is very attentive to their needs. However, when they are in mid-play with this very positive person, like little Albert experiencing the loud bang upon touching the rat, the child may experience punishment in the form of the loving mother being sent away. And the abusive mother coming into the room, abusing and therefore traumatising the alter who is present. This is designed to confuse and begin the foundations of programming, by encouraging the inside people to trust no one as they do not know who is safe and who is not.

BF Skinner (1948) also studied psychology from a behaviourist perspective and discovered that negative reinforcement and punishment could be used to modify the behaviour of the subject being studied. Negative reinforcement encourages certain types of behaviour because it removes an unpleasant experience or punishment that has been given. For systems of inside people, this can take the form of submissiveness, whereby the DID systems almost 'bow' to the mighty power of their programmers to stop the physical, ritual, sexual, mental or emotional abuse that is being perpetrated against them. Again, for tiny child alters, they may be made to feel that the abuse they receiving is their fault, to the point that they will do anything to make the violence and mind games stop. This is usually perpetrated by the abusive 'family members' of the coven, who are far removed from the love and care that the loving 'family members' may exhibit. The foundations are then laid for the children inside the system to have double binds presented to them. Indeed, these kinds of aforementioned behaviours are the most basic, and yet at the same time the most complex form of double binds that a child may ever receive.

A double bind occurs where two situations are presented to a DID system, both of which are negative and abusive in nature and which enhance trauma, but the child has to choose one of them just to survive the ordeals that they are experiencing. This method of programming not only blackmails the victim concerned into complying with their abusers, whichever choice they make, but it also very often takes away their voices.

Within our system our ten-year old twins, Charisma and Cathartic, were given the double binds of either being beaten and facing the prospect of becoming sex kittens (described later in this chapter), or becoming forensic experts, who were taught to cleanse crime scenes with expert capabilities, or they were threatened that the blame for the crime would be placed entirely on them, and the police would put them in prison. While this example of a double bind could almost be called a 'triple bind', it is still an intrinsic method of controlling by experimental mind control, and very often, leads to confusion and a very submissive attitude of alters who are desperate to please their coven masters at all costs. Unfortunately, however, these kinds of techniques are very often used in conjunction with hypnosis, which presents much more of a problem as the post-hypnotic suggestions that are used usually become much more ingrained in the victim's unconscious mind.

Within the world of ritual abuse and mind control, the use of hypnosis is highly prevalent when programming is been carried out on DID systems. We have friends overseas with DID, particularly in America, who have been through similar experiences to our own, showing that ritual abuse is a global issue and is not just centred in the UK. When using the principles of hypnosis in experimental mind control, it usually begins to be used very early in a child's life. When this begins, hypnosis is usually fostered through the use of everyday toys, which leave a child dissociative. One example of this is spin programming, in which children can be forced to look at a spinning top, and sometimes even a kaleidoscope, as they move in a circular motion, which is an integral part of the beginnings of spin programming. Once the child has been made to look at these toys for long periods of time, they become dissociative because of the continual pressure from the master programmer to become the one who is spinning, which then allows for the child to be hypnotised and for post-hypnotic suggestions to be used, which in a figurative sense turns the child into a spinning top. Literal upside-down spinning is then added into the mix, and then the initial programming is complete. From these experiences, once the child is spinning themselves by making small circular motions with their body, system-wide post-hypnotic suggestions can be made to the whole system which encourages a system-wide desire for suicide or for shutting down the system.

For our system, the spinning top was red, the kaleidoscope was multi-coloured, and the literal spinning which took place did so from the stone garage roof. A little child, tiny in fact, was taken behind the blue garage doors and spun until she thought that she was going to die. Accompanied by alternating beatings and other traumas, she collapsed, and when she came round, she did so to a hypnosis session incorporating post-hypnotic inductions which maimed her for life. After this happened, she was behaving as a spinning top, who was always spinning and never stopped, which is so sad for us all on the light side of our system, who want her to heal.

A post-hypnotic suggestion is something which happens once the victim is hypnotised, and gives instructions for what is to happen after the end of the hypnosis session. Within 'normal' life this can be used with great effectiveness on a clinical level, for example aiding with the cessation of smoking, however within the mind control circuit it can be used with evil intentions. One way of placing the DID system under programming conditions is through the use of psychic surgery. In everyday conditions, psychic surgery can eliminate the need for a general anaesthetic in operating-theatres, but for victims of experimental mind control, this is used in a very different way. After the child has been hypnotised, it is then possible for coven programmers to 'perform' internalised 'surgery' upon their victims by using post-hypnotic suggestions, which have a highly detrimental effect upon the alter(s) concerned. Again, by applying behaviourist principles of negative reinforcement and punishment, hypnosis provides a method of

Figure 1: A visualisation of the hypnosis process

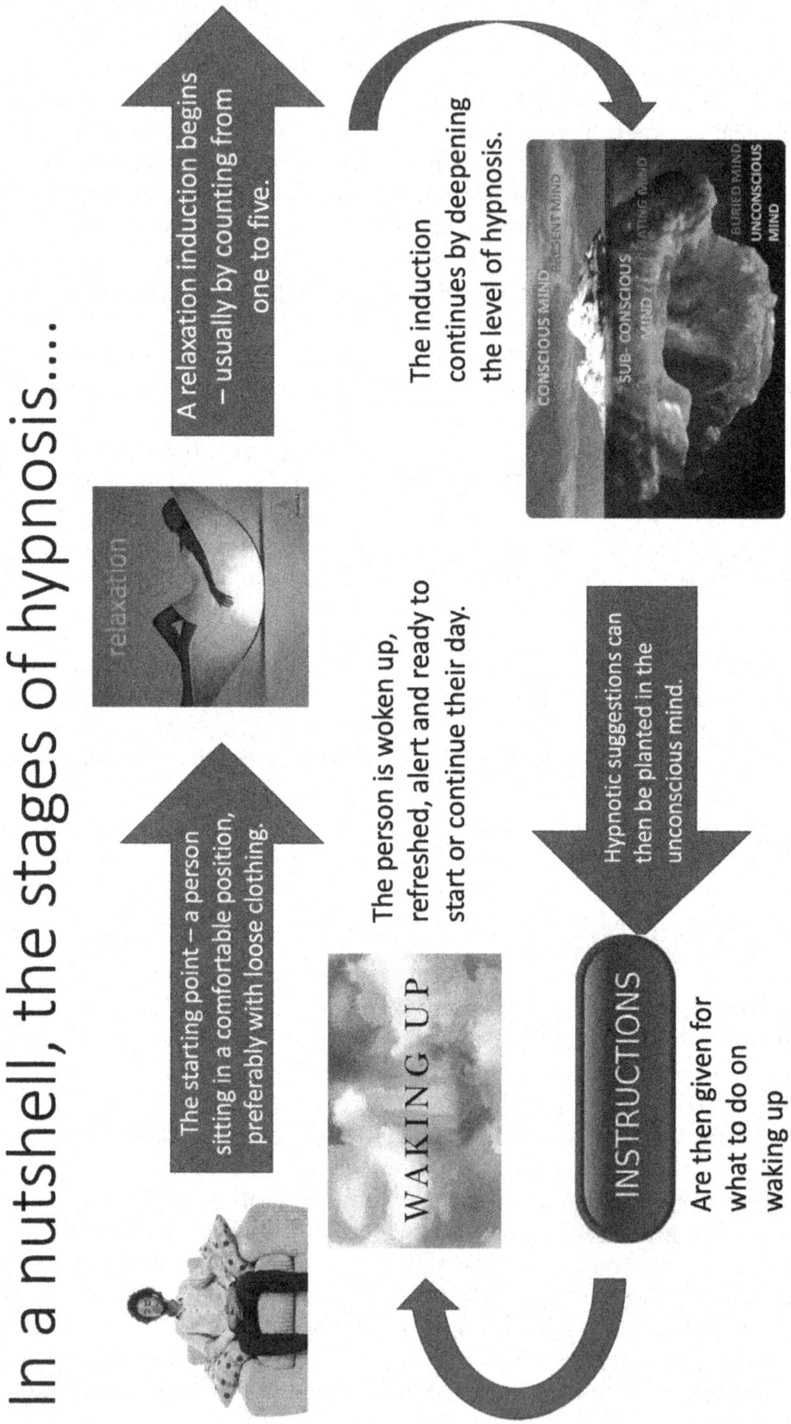

extreme punishment whereby the DID system, over a period of time, can become maimed, the belief being, for life. Within our system of the dancing dolphins, we have alternate personalities, who have been programmed in this way to deliberately send them blind by using psychic surgery to 'detach' their retinas, and another alter who is profoundly disabled as a result. As harsh as this sounds, people who are susceptible to hypnosis, of which children are highly so, will believe whatever the programmer says in these kinds of post-hypnotic inductions because they are in an altered state of consciousness.

For us, post-hypnotic suggestions started as a clinical hypnosis session would, quiet sounds, empathetic and surrounding us in a warm golden light. We were asked to watch our thoughts pass like clouds in the sky, and it all felt quite positive. It is only after deepening the hypnotic trance state by counting from one to five with increasing references to going to sleep, that we remember nothing of the session. We can only assume that other alters were created through terror and torture in this way during this time, as every time we try to think about what happened, we hear frightened children screaming and crying, and we can hear the pain in their cries. Some of them do not even have names, rather they have alpha numeric designations, which were given to them by their hypnotisers. The designations they have been given are symptomatic of Greenbaum programming. They each signify a type of alter and are named after the Greek alphabet, for example 'alpha' being general interference programmed alters which are designed to cause internal conflict and confusion, and 'beta' being sex kitten alters who are designed to pander to their customers' sexual desires, whilst the numbers are given to specific alters, meaning that they can be called out by anyone who knows the correct designation of the required inside person. This programming was developed by Dr Greenbaum, a German doctor working in the Second World War, and causes much fear and terror for many survivors of ritual abuse and experimental mind control. There is, however, a totally different type of programming involving forced dissociation, which creates alters that are not always born of trauma.

'Out of body experiences', are very often used by programmers to create alters, who are very often more loyal towards the coven than inside people who are created by trauma. Through the use of traumatic experiences, which are deliberately perpetrated to produce a causal effect of extreme terror, the abusers then encourage alters to split into further new alters by the original alter in the body, watching their body from the ceiling, looking down on it as it were. This allows room for new alters to enter the body because in forcing an alter on the ceiling via traumatic circumstances, deliberate dissociation occurs and someone new has to come along to fill the gap in time. This new alter may only be in the body for minutes or hours, but they can be manipulated to be loyal to the coven and be called upon to do coven tasks because other alters do not know of their existence. This is why alters can be 'dark' in persuasion as it is all that they have ever known. In our experience, we have alters who were forced into this type of dissociation, who were programmed into emulating Satan, their abusers and perpetrating crimes for their masters within their coven. For the host of our system, this causes a great deal of fear and shame that abusive alters are within the system, but our abusers did not care about the consequences, letting her continue to feel this way every day of our lives.

Moving onto the more formative years of the body's life, one experimental form of mind control that was used on us was 'Alice in Wonderland' programming. From a very young age, 'out of body experiences' were used on alters within our system to form further alters who were the very embodiment of people within the coven, one primary individual being the high priestess of our Satanic cult. The high priestess then slotted in as the 'quite mad' Queen of Hearts, with us as Alice (if you know the story of Alice in Wonderland by Lewis Carroll (1865)). This type of programming begins by establishing eating disorder mind control, whereby little ones eat food to make themselves big, and teenagers eat something else, and either binge and purge, or starve themselves to make themselves small again, to go through the internal doors within the DID system programmes concerned. Hereon in, the Mad Hatter's tea party is used to symbolise persecutory alters accusing an innocent Alice, to drive her quite insane, whilst the Queen of Hearts within our system is designed to trigger 'End Time', or 'Omega', programming by crying out 'off with her head', thus triggering a system-wide spin programme to kill off the body, as it is deemed a liability to the coven.

At the time of writing this chapter we are locked in a battle with the 'mad queen' and the 'mad hatter tea party' phases of the programming simultaneously attacking us. Internal persecutor alters are trying to instigate and goad the 'mad queen' to initiate the 'end time' programming, which is laid down in the System of the Dancing Dolphins. However, when this is combined with our spin programming, it can be interesting to note that programmes can very often be intrinsically linked to each other, all with the same potential outcomes – to cause general interference to the DID system's lives, to cause sex kitten behaviours and traits within the system, and to kill our whole system. To name but just a few avenues of mind control.

Another form of story-based programming is 'Wizard of Oz' programming (Frank-Baum & Langley, 1900). In the story of the Wizard of Oz, the central character follows a yellow brick road pursued by an evil witch, until she takes some characters along with her for courage, a heart and a brain. This story is used with great effect by master programmers, who use the story to symbolise aspects of mind control. The central character, Dorothy, follows the yellow brick road with her companions, which is symbolic of all alters following the host and/or core person in the system down the 'road' of the programming. When Dorothy and her companions fall asleep in the poppy fields, this symbolises the omega or end time programming causing human fatalities, and when the central character and her companions arrive at Oz, everything is green symbolising Dr Greenbaum's programming. The lack of courage, a heart and a brain, thus seals the victim's fate, of having a controlled mind and heart, and because of hypnosis, a distinct lack of courage. This story is usually used to programme young children, but can also be used into the teenage years, and can even be modified if still subject to ritual abuse much later in life.

When looking to the ten to 12-year-old and teenage age brackets of a DID system, it is still possible to programme the young alters, since they have learned to be and indeed are susceptible to the mind control that is already ingrained within the system. Master mind control programmers do not stay wholly based in the past, but rather adapt to suit their mind control techniques to whatever is going on in the wider world at the time. For us, adapting to trends in television cultures, another experimental form of mind control that was used was 'Borg Programming'.

Borg programming has some interesting features that, although they relate largely to older programming methods, they have a uniqueness about them which can make a whole DID system's lives change for the worst, or, without therapy, forever. In the television series 'Star Trek: The Next Generation', their exists a race of beings called the Borg. The Borg Queen, similar in some regards to the queen in a hive of bees, assimilates innocent people into her way of thinking, so they only do her bidding and hear her voice in their heads. The Borg are enhanced by robotic features, and only rest when they are told to, and like an automaton, they carry out robotic tasks as if unknowing of what they are doing. They can also be physically violent if people disagree with their actions, or resist and challenge them.

Within our system, experimental programming was created around the Borg systems, delegations and mechanisms, in a manner very reminiscent of the characters in the 'Star Trek' programme, as detailed above. In likeness to 'Alice in Wonderland' programming, The Borg Queen is an alter, born from the attributes of the Satanic high priestess, and speaks directly into the minds and thoughts of different alters within the system. Hence assimilating them into the coven ways of thinking, such as end-time or omega programming. Each alter has a numeric designation, not dissimilar to Greenbaum programming, except for the notion that each 'drone', as each person is known, is divided into subgroups, which form a whole system, all dependent on the 'Borg Queen' for every command and action. So when Borg programming is active, random alters may turn into an automaton-like state, following an unknown commander, and, as alters are assimilated, more and more of the system may begin a transition from traumatised alters into drones whose primary aim is to follow their internal Queen. Borg systems, however, do have their own self-destruct system whereby, if the system is deemed to be a liability, it is designed to commit suicide as quickly as possible, thus 'blowing up' their entire operation.

There are also facets of 'Borg programming' that are designed to assimilate other people outside the DID system into their way of thinking. Borg alters can turn people who are susceptible to hypnosis into singular drones, hence the need for 24-hour support to be available for the rest of the DID system's lives. If this support is not available, singleton programmed drones can be used to commit crimes including violent crimes, that remain unknown to the police who can never reach the source who inspired or ordered the crime. Therapy too, can take many long years to heal drones within a DID system, as, in a system like ours, there may be thousands of fragmented and whole alters within it, all of whom are dependent on the voice of the Borg Queen. This therefore shows the need for better education and awareness within the NHS and the police in particular, so that these victims can be identified and properly supported.

It is dreadful that people such as experimental programmers within covens can take fictional television shows and turn them into effective ways of controlling a person's mind. Even watching the shows unknowingly can trigger responses between unknown alters within a DID system, which can have a damaging effect on the whole group of alters. This concurs with evidence used by Bandura (1977) in his Social Learning Theory in which violent television shows can have a controlling and detrimental effect on children who may go on to exhibit violent behaviour, including young alters, who are children themselves. Although the discussion above concerns the new programming of singleton adults as opposed to those in DID systems, it can still be argued that people who are susceptible to hypnosis, regardless of their age, can still be mind-controlled. This presents vulnerabilities to DID systems trying to assimilate people into becoming drones, as in not knowing who they are encountering, they could be harmed by people who may already be dangerous themselves. In continuing the programming in a very 'underground' manner, and by continually watching the aforementioned television show, more and more alters can become drones without even realising what is happening, thus further damaging and retraumatising the DID system concerned.

Following on from 'Borg' programming, is an extension of the 'Star Trek' story line-based mind control, known as experimental 'Nemesis', programming. Nemesis is the name of a 'Star Trek' movie in which alien cultures create clones of the main officer of the Star Trek team and discover an android which was in turn recreated by another android from scattered broken parts. For us in the system of the Dancing Dolphins (and we have no doubt that this is the same for other people with DID and programming), Nemesis programming has two experimental facets of mind control which were used on us with great effect.

First is the notion of cloning. Quite early on in our therapy we discovered a cloning room inside our system, which we now know comes from Nemesis programming. The nemesis that can be found here is that, without careful therapy to eliminate the cloning room in DID systems, dark alters can be created through internalised hypnosis procedures, which can be mistaken for real traumatised alters, except for the fact that they do not carry the true memories of the original alters who experienced the primary traumas themselves. Like the cloning of the Star Trek officer in the movie 'Nemesis', cloning can be designed to confuse and discredit the authentic alters to the authorities. For example the police can be confused, which in turn can prevent the system from being believed, which can stop the programming offenders who put the mind control in place from being caught. They are not specialist trained in mind control.

The second facet of mind control which has a negative impact on the system is the notion of an android, robot-like man recreating another robotic android. First, this part of the story line was used with our system to internally symbolise the master programmer recreating a 'tabula rasa' blank slate baby, into a system of traumatised people. On deeper examination, however, through therapy, we have come to realise that our ultimate nemesis is the extension of the Borg programming creating drones or automaton alters which are robotic alters created by robotic alters being released into our system. What this means for the DID system concerned, is that the whole system can be changed and recreated and grow into something which is a whole new programming conundrum for the therapist supporting them.

We used to have what our system called 'stone people' inside our system who were hypnotised and spoke very sleepily and without moving, seemingly in a permanent trance-like state. What we have learned however transcends this limited knowledge of our system. What we are discovering from internal system sources is that these are the side effects of someone who has been Borg programmed by another person of Borg culture and that assimilation into the Borg culture is essentially trying to make a clone out of an authentic alter. Thus, the whole system can stay in a trance-like state which in turn discredits them to police officers and NHS funders alike. This can be hugely detrimental to a system with this type of programming, as without a knowledgeable therapist or psychologist providing input on the DID system's behalf, support can be found to be unneeded, simply because people do not understand the complexity of the mind control which is happening to the survivors concerned.

Borg programming can very often be used in conjunction with a number of other programmes, and with our system this was carried out with additional forms of mind control that were in their most experimental forms. It seems to be the case that after the beginnings of Greenbaum programming which began mainly in the Second World War, experimental programming became more and more refined and sophisticated, and became extensions of mind control forms that had gone before. Like the alpha numerical designations of Greenbaum programming, Borg programming had numerical designations. Bringing this right forward to the present day, ISIS terrorists are trained like soldiers but with elements of brainwashing and mind control, which, like the use of the ideology of Satanism, uses a corrupted and extreme form of the ideology of the

Muslim faith. These people are the forward thinkers of mind-control, and while they are only a minority of people practising these extreme ideologies, they offer a much-needed educative opportunity for the authorities.

In our lives, we have had a very tumultuous time trying to report our experiences to the police. Due to our programming we have had many difficulties, such as a screen alter trying to let the police know that everything is OK when the rest of us know that this is very much not the case. Screen alters are programmed into a DID system to discredit and sow disbelief amongst the police and authorities, by acting as a screen which metaphorically obscures the truth of the ritual abuse, along with hiding evidence deep within the system, imprisoned where only through therapy can it again be exposed to the light. This also shows that there is a need amongst programming-trained authorities to expose the criminals who perpetrate these crimes, whether it be historic abuse or present.

There are many facets to mind control, all of which can be used to mask the abusers, and can assist in hiding them from the police. There are many tasks that can be given to a system that makes them appear to be criminals in nature, except for the fact that if they were not programmed they would not be committing any crimes at all. Alters may be called upon to become sex workers as previously discussed, be forced into becoming 'breeders', having children for the exclusive use of the coven, or even may be called upon to assist in killing someone who has broken the code of silence required by covens and cults across the world. As we have discovered, they may be forced into forensic cleansing or even to perform detrimental psychic surgery. The real injustice in these situations is that unless these experimental programmes are found to be in existence via careful therapy, these inside people who are innocent of all blame may never know what has happened to them, thus never fully heal from ritual abuse and mind control.

We, as a DID system, and others all across the world, have experienced a great deal of trauma and pain as a result of the programming which binds us to criminals, sometimes for life. It is only with specialist therapy and a safe place to live, away from covens and cults, that mind control can be unravelled and a degree of healing can take place. We say a degree of healing because, with all of the complexities of mind control, full healing and the wish of many people with DID to integrate, may not happen due to the complexities of their system. What can happen, however, is that a meaningful life can be developed for all alters, with support, and with that a degree of fulfilment and normality can be achieved for every alter.

## References

Watson JB and Raynor R (1920) 'conditioned emotional reaction', *Journal of Experimental Psychology* **3**, 1-14.

Skinner BF (1948) *Operant conditioning*. 2017. London: Routledge.

Skinner BF (1974) *About Behaviourism.* New York: Vintage Books.

Hammond DC (1992) *The Greenbaum lecture*. Mark Center, Alexandria, Virginia, USA.

Carroll L (1865) *Alice in Wonderland.* London: Macmillan.

Baum F (1900) *The Wonderful Wizard of Oz.* Chicago: George M. Hill Company.

Bandura A (1977) *Social Learning Theory*. Englewood Cliffs: Prentice Hall.

# Chapter 5: The complexities of a DID system: experiencing forced dissociation

Carrie Anne Smith

Classic dissociation in Dissociative Identity Disorder (DID) is in essence a response to very severe trauma. Within a DID system, an 'alter' (alternate personality) is born to trauma by part of the personality splitting off from the whole to form a new identity, with his or her own pattern of thinking and perception of the world (American Psychiatric Association, 2013). Alters are also born at the age that the trauma occurred, which can make for a vast number of ages within one DID system, depending on the trauma that they were subjected to. Alters also have completely different senses of self, may be male, female or even animal in persuasion, and all alters will have their own likes and dislikes; for example, in our DID system, I, the host, have a liking for tuna mayonnaise, but another alter in my system who is six years old cannot stand it!

Within these DID systems, there are also alters who are 'light' and 'dark side' in nature. This makes for even greater complexities within groups of alters, because those of a light nature want to heal, change and grow, and indeed heal from their traumas, whereas the alters who are 'dark' sided are, in our experience, very coven-loyal, and take a lot of therapy to realise that they have a choice about whether they remain loyal to their abusers, or whether they come to the light, face what happened to them and move on to healing. These alters are very often born of forced dissociation, but also can come about as a result of some of the most severe trauma that the system experiences.

This goes back to the double dissociative babies (installed DID) mentioned in chapter three. Due to their lack of basic needs being met (as defined by Maslow and his hierarchy of needs (1943)), combined with a lack of 'good enough parenting' (Winnicott, 1953), which is continued through primary and secondary socialisation, this double dissociative-ness can persist beyond childhood and continue into later life. This encapsulates both alters left from when the child was a double dissociative baby, and alters born later in life, surviving through the many traumas that they go on to experience without their needs being met.

In many people's DID systems there is a core person with the name the body was given at birth, who, in adulthood, does the kind of things that keep real life going, for example paying bills and doing the weekly food shop. This keeps a certain degree of continuity and normality in life. It helps the core person, who may be a lot older than his or her alters, to look after them after a time in therapy, and keep them safe. They can make decisions that affect the whole system, such as about their body's health the way a parent would over a child. Our system, however, is made up of a vast collection of alters, born both naturally of trauma and forced dissociation and mind control. This means that, with no core person, I, the host, am 19 years of age but the body is much older, which would be the age of the core person, if we had one.

It is important to consider the fact that although mind control may incorporate many traumas and abuses of all natures, and almost always has a co-morbidity with Satanist Ritual Abuse, by the very nature of how it is ingrained in a system's psyche, the most horrific traumas can come from laying down mind programming in the system itself. This means that classic dissociation almost certainly occurs when mind programming is taking place on a victim and it can therefore almost always be argued that the natural trauma that occurs from this goes on to perpetuate the mind control through the rest of the victim's lives.

In order to understand how this phenomenon takes place, it is essential to clarify the physical, mental and emotional facets of mind control and how they are used to create the perfect mind-controlled slave. To start with, programming usually begins at a very young age, using toys, nursery rhymes and psychological techniques such as those of behaviourism, and more specifically the application of extinction, whereby the child's basic needs to survive e.g. food and shelter, are taken away, so the child eventually stops expecting to ever have them (Skinner, 1948), and this was used prolifically in our case. All of this conditioning, words and objects being used, are applied together, to cause the child to become used to, and readily accept, being subjected to hypnosis and the use of post – hypnotic inductions, which are a set of predefined phrased words that takes a person, or in our case child alters, into a state of somnambulism, also known as hypnosis.

But where does the trauma come in? Stanley Milgram (1974) conducted an experiment involving participants being told to give increasing levels of electric shocks to an innocent man in another room whenever he got a question, which was asked of him by the participants, incorrect. The electric shocks were not actually applied to the man in the other room, but the participants were led to believe that they were and that they had to give the shocks to the man. Whilst this experiment was highly unethical, it does offer a good insight into the nature of the traumas that children go through, in forced co-operation, concordance and co-ordination with their abusers. Like the participants in Milgram's experiment, some of which purported to be controlled and traumatised by it, the control exerted on children during programming can be used to the extent that they are made to watch people being killed or be torturously abused, including people they love, and are made to believe it is their fault. They can also be silenced into never speaking of what happened or what they have witnessed. This means that, like Milgram's study, where participants purported to be traumatised, alters can stay traumatised, unable to heal from the constant traumas that are inflicted upon them, or they can turn loyal to the Satanic coven in an attempt to gain the approval of the leaders, thus finding a way to make the abuse stop.

In our case, one example of this involved a child alter who is six. As part of her programming, she was forced to watch someone she loved literally being shot in a field, and was told it was all her fault. This incorporates behavioural notions of the extinction of the relationship, the mental trauma of witnessing a murder, whilst emotionally blackmailing and controlling her into silence, and thus scarring her for life. After this happened, her master, the coven hypnotiser, applied the use of a toy spinning top and a nursery rhyme to bring about a post-hypnotic induction to make her remember with terror this trauma, to further dissociate, and programme her into automatically shutting down to facilitate omega, end-time, or suicide programming.

Our six year old and what she witnessed caused natural and classic dissociation and terror. What she experienced afterwards however, was far from natural. The coven hypnotiser deliberately traumatised her by the use of hypnosis, intentionally deepening the dissociation she had experienced. This is also a similar and yet different form of double dissociation. Our child alter concerned actually experienced an intermingling of natural dissociative stimulation, combined with that of a forced nature, which in turn traumatised and dissociated her in a double nature.

There are other alters, who, whilst being born of dissociation, are of a totally forced nature and are therefore less 'natural' than the more 'classic' types of dissociation. These are alters created by techniques such as hypnosis, split brain work and the 'out of body experiences' that are mentioned in chapter three. They are alters who are usually created for specific jobs within their DID system, such as those who report a system's activities back to the coven, or those who are used for sex work – named sex kittens within the coven. It should be noted that the roles they inhabit are predefined by the coven handlers involved in programming the system.

For us, this took the form of Greenbaum programming which involves the use of hypnosis, alpha numerical designations for alters and their roles following the Greek alphabet, instead of the names many more natural alters have, and torture to force the dissociation. Drugging was also used during this form of mind control. Programming in our system also involved out of body experiences, whereby alters were taught to watch what was happening to them whilst being on the ceiling, thus deepening the dissociation that these 'forced' alters actually had. We were also subjected to split brain work during which the brain was literally split in a psychological way so the body did not engage with the world in a biologically correct manner. Alters were placed in left and right brain settings deliberately in order to create a lack of continuity or connection in the system so that different alters on different sides of the brain never encountered each other and amnesiatic barriers were thus formed between alters; one of our protectors remembers this taking place, and there were two voices in his head at the same time, hypnotising him with two post-hypnotic inductions at the same time, one in the left brain and one in the right. Finally, experimental forms of programming such as 'Alice in Wonderland' programming took place, where the host of the system (Alice) is controlled by the queen (the satanic coven's 'High Priestess') into killing herself after hearing the queen's voice in her head, telling her to do so (as in the story crying "off with her head" (Carroll, 1865)), were also used on us with great effect. This is one example of a complex experimental form of omega, end time or suicide mind control programming.

As previously defined, one primary programme that we have is end time programming, also known as suicide or omega programming, of which Alice in Wonderland programming is one example. The main aim is for the coven to mind control DID systems into believing that it is of the utmost importance that they kill their own body. This is so the system's death appears to be suicide, and avoids the need for the coven to commit murder. This coven-programmed form of protection is sadly a life-long mind control condition, as even when not running it is always there, and involves both classically dissociated alters and those who were forced into dissociation. This means that, like a long-term chronic health condition, adjustments need to be made to learn to accept and live with the programme and within its constraints.

Forced dissociation is rife in programmes such as end time. Within our system there are alters who were created to do specific jobs within the programmes, and who only become active when it is time to fulfil their role. This means that the particular alters concerned were forced through torture, hypnosis and out of body experiences, to submit to anything the programmers told them to do. In our system there are children desperate to please, who are trained through mind control programming to start end time programming off, like the aforementioned six year old, by shutting down, and then teenagers are mind controlled into carrying out the selves ultimate end time, by ending the body's life, and like the candle that lights the clock face, when something goes wrong, the light goes out.

If, however, the mind control programme becomes inactive then we have alters who are trained by the coven to re-hypnotise younger children and teenagers within our system to continue the programming, so it becomes active again. Our internal landscape is a very visual one, so this is done via visualisation of alters involved being a system of cogs and gears, like those in an old-fashioned clock tower. There are young children who look after switches to change the way that the cogs and gears work, but they are so terrified by the forced dissociation they encountered that they dare not use the switches that will turn the programmes off, or indeed change the way in which they work. This means a lot of work in therapy to help them realise that it is now safe for them to change their minds.

We also used to have alters who were created by forced dissociation who our system named 'screen alters'. The name 'screen alters', to our system specifically, denotes the fact that these alters in particular acted to screen and hide the truth, and portrayed a played-out television screen of normality to the rest of the world. These inside people were created to make the system look normal, even to the authorities, if they are ever involved. They were also programmed to know nothing of the rest of the system and their history, therefore negating and discrediting anything that the rest of us said to other people. It is only through therapy that these alters have become obsolete, and being unneeded because our truths are finally being told, they have dissipated and no longer exist within the system.

The forced dissociation experienced by screen alters involved taking a natural dissociative state of losing time, combined with the use of hypnosis, so that alters only remember normal things that happen in life, and not the terror and the trauma. This can be likened to having an old cassette tape with a recording of a complete song on it. If someone comes along and wipes a huge portion of the song so that only the chorus is left, anyone listening would believe that this is the sum total of the song (assuming the listener has never heard the song before). So, through the use of lost time and hypnosis, alters are forced into being with such a deep degree of dissociation that they only remember 'normal' parts of life, like the aforementioned tape recording with only the chorus remaining.

What does this mean to a DID system with forced dissociated alters and trauma-created and stimulated alters? It means that life for these systems is not a life – they are trapped in a non-life. One of the hardest things for a system to acknowledge and admit to themselves is that they are all trapped in a mind control maze, like rats trapped in a skinner box maze (Skinner, 1948) looking for the right route to find food. However, with the mind control 'maze', alters are pitted against each other. Each of the forced dissociative alters are clinging to their roles, be that end time or screen training, or being a sex kitten, while others are clinging to survive and desperate to heal from their trauma somehow. All of these alters are in a fight for their own lives and only therapy can help them. Even then, though, mind control is a life-long condition. A non-life – a monotone life that is completely at the mercy of the mind controller.

In our system, we find it hard to accept that we can never be free of mind control. We want it to be gone so we can enjoy the same activities of daily living that any 'normal' person can. It is important to remember, though, that whether be it alters born of natural dissociation or forced dissociation, all of them need to heal and accept the situation that they find themselves in. Some therapists aim to heal victims by deprogramming the DID system affected using techniques such as re-hypnotising, with the aim to disable alters born of forced dissociation who may be troublesome and/or coven loyal, in particular. This did not work for us, however, as we are very complex. In fact, if anything, this did us a lot of damage as it compounded the programming that was already laid down. For our system, working in therapy long term with regular sessions with our psychologist works best, as there are so many of us to share our stories that it takes some time, and there are always 'new' alters coming forward with their own traumas. Also, because there are such a wide and varied number of alters (in fact numbering thousands in total, including fragmented alters, both light and dark side, and naturally born of trauma along with those created by forced dissociation) there are still a great many alters right at the beginning of their healing journey.

For us, there are so many alters in our system that a large number exist in an unconscious layer, as well as in the conscious. Mind control defined where they would reside within our system, namely hypnosis for the main part, but through therapy and an urgent need to come out and be heard, a number of alters are flooding their way into our consciousness. For some DID systems, the flooding of alters and memories is a phenomenon born of natural, classic dissociation, however for us the response to programming is a part laid down and another part is an internally created programme through an alter called 'the internal programmer', and is termed a 'flooder' programme. Flooder types of mind control are deliberately laid down in people's DID systems, and are designed to flood the system with so many alters and memories that a system cannot cope, which in turn initiates end time, omega or suicide programming. This is why there are so many alters coming out to flood the system – and with a deadly reason, there is no wonder that it inspires fear in the hearts of all our alters who are currently in the conscious realm.

A complex system's response to mind control is to naturally dissociate, but with programmes such as the flooders the mind control causes the dissociation by reinforcing the split brain work of separating neural pathways between alters, which, in turn, causes the dissociation to be perpetuated. This is the complex interplay of dissociation and mind control. Neural pathways connect alters to each other within the brain, both physically and mentally, so there is a level of co-consciousness, however split brain work deliberately destroys these, so alters are unaware of each other. The effects of split brain work are far reaching and can even cause dissociation from the biological body, causing some alters to have disabilities, for example, such as blindness, while others in the same system don't. So imagine if you can, with empathy, the effect of blindness upon an alter's reoccurring trauma: it will compound and deepen the depth of dissociation experienced as a result of the trauma, which will in turn further weaken the neural pathways between synapses (which fire the messages between different parts of the brain) that connect the body and selves in the DID system to others on the opposite side of the brain, thereby impacting on links between different alters, or preventing those links from being forged.

Split brain work can also be used in conjunction with psychic surgery. This in essence involves the use of hypnosis to, in a Satanist coven, harm people by the using deeply traumatising hypnotic 'surgery', which leaves a victim believing, for example, they no longer have any legs or that the auditory canals in their body have been removed. For this system, the hypnotic inductions always started out as if the subject was in a normal clinical hypnosis session, but turned out as being hugely traumatic, thus causing further parts of the body to dissociate and shut down.

Psychic surgery in it's true form involves physical surgery that takes place in an operating theatre but, where a subject may not be able to have an anaesthetic, it can be done using hypnosis. This is carried out with qualified personnel who are trained in what they are doing. The type of surgery, however, is simulated very accurately, until the mind control takes bodily functions away from people. Here the side affects are for the mind and body to deeply dissociate, and, like split brain work, neural pathways connecting the brain to the body are lost or damaged so, unless it is worked through in therapy, these connections can remain lost forever; for example, we have an alter who is blind because his optic nerves were cut using psychic surgery, and it remains the same indefinitely for him currently, because he has not worked through his afflictions in therapy. This, however, is a long process, and our alter has only just started his therapeutic journey.

As it is clear to see, dissociation is the only way to survive when you are 'stitched up', as one of my alters has just said, by mind control, and this is a very apt response to it. The mind is very creative, and dissociation can be seen as a very adaptive and logical response to trauma. Out of body experiences, and dissociation, for example, lessen the impact of the trauma on the brain, as without it, the brain would literally end up psychotic, psychopathic or some such other intense psychological condition. There are many ways in which the brain can cope as a response to mind control, using hypnosis, however, and some of them can provide a helpful intervention to stressors and re-traumatising events, such as flashbacks and somatic memories.

Within our DID system is a subsystem called 'the dancers'. When these alters were being badly abused, they used to imagine themselves as dancing movements of all genres, to get them through the traumas that they were facing. This was then perpetuated as more and more fragmented alters were born as a result of trauma, on top of the original dancer as a result of recurring traumas, and they then became a subsystem, or team of alters, who worked together to get through the atrocities that they were facing. Nowadays however these alters provide a welcome distraction to everyday stressors and memories, because when mind control takes over we can see them dancing inside the system. It is beautiful to watch, and we are grateful to them for doing this for us, as the response to mind control is now being used in a positive way, to help us get through life.

Another way in which we as a system cope with the ongoing effects of mind control is by dissociating into music. Music to many people is seen as therapeutic and a way to access pleasurable emotions, but for our DID system, this is taken one step further. If you imagine being able to lose yourself in music so much that you almost become the music, in a deeply and completely relaxed manner, and in a way that music almost becomes hypnotic, then you will be able to see the way in which we dissociate into music. Again, however, this helps strengthen neural pathways to the extent that music becomes more important than the mind control, which in turn helps to make new pathways that assist in the negation and destruction of the mind control. It is only through the making of new neural pathways within the brain that alters can learn to communicate to each other, and share healing experiences and make happy new memories with each other, and indeed of their own.

As a system, we have complex programming, to the degree that we can never integrate (become a whole person instead of just alters), and as a system we feel so scarred by the mind control that raped and stole our mind, that we feel like damaged goods. Even though we are learning about new aspects of our programming all the time and are gradually being imparted from alters who were picked for teaching coven folk how to programme others, it is still a hard and bitter pill to swallow. Programming has twisted and infringed every part of our lives, and a normal life is something that we can never have and never get back, and that leaves many of us feeling quite bitter. The only way we can hope to heal is by making new memories, with new and safe people we trust including attachment figures (Frankish & Sinason 2017) who we can talk to and pursue appropriate relationships with, and to tell of our experiences in the hope that it will help others. If we have one hope it is that we are able to show people that mind control happens, and mind control programming is real.

## References

American Psychiatric association (2013. *Diagnostic Statistical Manual-V*)

Maslow A H (1943) *A Theory of Human Motivation.* 2013. Eastford: Martino Fine Books.

Skinner BF (1948) *Operant conditioning.* 2017. London: Routledge.

Milgram S (1974) *Obedience to authority; an Experimental View.* New York: Harper & Roe.

Carroll L (1865) *Alice in Wonderland.* London: Macmillan.

Frankish P and Sinason V (2017) *Holistic Therapy for People with DID.* London: Routledge.

# Chapter 6: A voice from the inside

## Alistair / Protector

We were first initiated into the coven (another name for cult) by a six-year-old female alter. She witnessed the brutal murder of one of her loving coven mothers, of which she had several, but loved this one the most. The murder involved a horrific shooting, which our six-year-old was made to witness, and was then mind control programmed into believing that this was all her fault. This alter was then mind controlled using spin programming. This involved making her believe that she was a spinning top, by watching the toy of the same name, being hypnotised, and being spun by the ankles upside down from the garage roof of her home, all to fill her with terror and mind control her.

Not long after this happened, September 7th came along, which is the ritual date of the Marriage to the Beast – an annual coven ritual. Our six-year-old was initiated into the coven by 'marrying Satan', but her main initiation had already happened after the murder she witnessed. You see, this one event meant the coven had already predefined our role within the coven. We were to be trained in coven practices, to become a master programmer or trainer, and a high priestess in one Dissociative Identity Disorder (DID) system. This was what all of our programming and training was leading up to, even at this tender age.

You have already heard of trauma-based dissociation and that of a forced nature in previous chapters. Our six-year-old was being used in a double dissociative manner, by dissociation via trauma, and she was also the first of us (that we know of) to be used with forced dissociation. All of this made her a key alter in our system, as even at the age of six she was being trained into the foundations of omega, end time or suicide programming, and all due to the initiations of murder and 'marriage to the beast' rituals during which she was consummated by the coven. It was also these foundations that led me to the position that I now find myself in.

Fast forward to when the body was my age, aged fifteen years old. I never thought the coven would stitch me up, as a coven leader, so that only I would be caught by the police, while the rest of the members went underground. I, however, was born of trauma initially. One of our other bodily roles within the coven was to be a breeder, which is a DID system or person who gives birth to premature babies, who were deliberately induced early to be taken by the coven for taking their lives in Good Friday rituals. One of my predecessor alters had just given birth in one such ritual, and the trauma had been too much for her to cope with, and, finding myself slammed down to the floor at the end of giving birth, I was terrified. I did not have time to think however, because one of the most traumatic things that have ever happened to me came about and was to leave me never able to forgive myself.

The initiation of our six-year-old came full circle, with horrific consequences for me personally. I was told that, as a male alter, I had to have the balls to 'assist' with the taking of this baby's life. I yelled 'no', and tried to run away, but with a birth-weakened body that felt like jelly, I could not, and even though I tried to flail my arms at them in an effort to get free, I could not. I was soon placed in a vice-like grip that I could not get away from, and I was then subjected to mind control. You see, in such a traumatised state I was highly dissociative and so was easy to hypnotise. I remember nothing then, for what seemed like ages, but in reality it was not that long. The hypnosis was all to force me into a horrific initiation into my place in the coven. When that six-year-old all those years ago saw the murder, it predefined my system and more specifically forced me into the role of master trainer and another sacrificial ritual was my initiation. All of my (and indeed, our) training and mind control programming up to this point had been with a view to this initiation.

My forced dissociation culminated in the Good Friday ritual of the sacrifice of a baby, and afterwards I was hailed a murderer by the coven, and was told that if I told anyone I would be killed. In this one act that I was mind controlled into, I was trapped into a double bind of being very traumatised and guilty, with no hope of telling anyone, whilst I was hailed a prospective coven leader who could be easily trained into my role due to my susceptibility to hypnosis. This was a big choice for me to make. On the one hand, if I committed to the role of master programmer, I thought I could make the abuse stop as I would be pleasing the coven leaders. On the other hand I could not justify in my heart all of this hurt and coven murders that were taking place as a result of mind control. The coven had decided to use me as a coven leader in training, so I decided to go along with it, as it was the only way to try and find peace and acceptance.

After a short time where I was placed in a dog cage naked as punishment for being slow in deciding, I was soon to start the training that would come to place me in potentially very high standing within the coven. A trainer or programmer engages in a lot of techniques to mind control people. As well as behavioural techniques as mentioned in chapter four, and hypnosis, I was to go on to learn spin programming techniques, Greenbaum programming, split brain approaches, out of body experiences and twinning. To twin two alters together means that they are, in essence, separately experiencing the same experience or trauma, but they are doing it simultaneously using hypnosis, so that they are connected by neural pathways for specific coven reasons, namely to mind control and create alters who are twinned light to dark in nature, to create double binds within the system. I was also twinned with the head coven programmer via hypnosis, so that I knew what he knew.

Hypnosis was one of the earliest things I learnt. To learn that you have enough power over human beings to put them in life and death situations is scary. Hypnotic inductions like those mentioned in chapter four used to start off really innocent and relaxing for new members, but soon turned into something much more sinister in nature. For this training, I was twinned with the psychic surgeon, in our DID systems, as he was learning hypnosis with a view to him performing evil psychic surgery on other alters and human beings. I learnt how to speak and that you were to begin by relaxing your victim, to the extent that you feel that the victim you are hypnotising is fully comfortable with you. You then talk them into a double bind by stating that all human beings have the capacity to heal, change and grow.

After counting down from ten to one, gradually talking the victim into a hypnotic trance state with a gentle click of your fingers at each number point, they are then deeply and completely relaxed. It is then that things start to turn sinister and nasty. I was taught at this point that, in the same way that the psychic surgery team in the system were taught, to deepen even further the hypnosis state that the person was in by informing them that they could relax. Under hypnosis I made them believe they had been giving an anaesthetic, putting them into a state where they did not need to take notice of anything I said and to allow their thoughts to pass away like watching clouds in the sky. Once under the hypnotic anaesthetic, I tested the person to check that their state of somnambulism (trance state) was real by stating that they had a balloon tied to their wrist, and if when I told them to let the balloon float up, their right wrist would rise into the air, I knew the hypnotic process had worked.

Once all of this had taken place, the victim was prepared for the hypnotic suggestions. I would begin my programming phrases by saying, "You don't have to listen to anything I say, but…" and then I would begin placing the programming into their minds. One experimental programme that I was subjected to, and was made to use on others, was all concentrated on a new form of end time programming. Still a new form of mind control when I was taught it, I was made to hold my breath underwater, until I was practically unconscious, and then I was fished out of the water. This was all to show me how to simulate the hypnotic way to fool the autonomic nervous system and brain into thinking it did not need to breathe, until it was to a dangerous point at which the body could die. There was also a way of making a person fully reliant on the coven by placing them on a hypnotic ventilator, thus making all of their actions and their body at the discretion and control of the coven.

This was life for me, caught in the trap of being so mind controlled myself that I mind controlled others. At the same time, I was assisted externally by the head programmer, and internally by Celestine, the new high priestess in training. The current high priestess was nicknamed 'the gassing lady', because of her connections to both normal and hypnotic forms of anaesthetic, and Celestine was being trained to take over from her because of the current high priestess's age. Celestine could hypnotise people into trance states that were of a depth lower than mine, and was called upon to assist with particularly hard to hypnotise people, as she had the kind of lingo and voice that would cause people to 'spark out'.

Whilst Celestine was very good at hypnosis, she was not called upon to spin programme people. This may seem a little strange, but it was because although she had excellent hypnotic skills, she lacked the brute force that was needed to lift people onto the physical spinning device in the garage, so I was called upon to do this. This was because some of the alters in our system have physical disabilities that others do not, and Celestine was one of them, but anyway, males were classed as more important in covens we went to, so I was higher up the pecking order than her.

Generally, children were spin programmed rather than adults, and even though people could be in a trance state before being placed on the spinning device, they were still a dead weight to lift. This was one of the forms of torture that I did not like doing though, as it was a form of torture that left people so compliant that they would do anything for me, and that was something I did not want to happen. I wanted them to fight me, in fact, because at this point I was beginning at times to feel guilty for what I was doing. The problem was, however, that whenever I said I wanted to stop doing these things I was threatened with what happened when I 'assisted' my predecessor alter's baby's sacrifice.

I was taught nearly all of the mind control processes that were done on this system. To be able to do it though, my mind had to further and further dissociate to be able to carry out my predefined task of training people. That was the only way in which I could cope with mind controlling my victims. You see, even mind controllers have generally been through programming themselves to get them where they are. That is no excuse for what they do, of course, and I will never forgive the people who programmed me, or be able to forgive myself for the hurt I was trained to inflict on innocent children and adults, both externally, and internally within the system.

Celestine and I were programmed in the use of split brain work too, and for my part, I was twinned when being trained in it, with our internal psychologist, who was put in our system by the coven by means of forced dissociation. The psychologist was taught psychological components that were used in programming and this was the reason he was also trained to understand neural pathways and everything that goes with this type of programming. I was involved in my own split brain work however, as apart from a little internal contact with Celestine, I had no neural pathways with anyone inside, and I know this because when I was around I lost a lot of time, and I could never hear anyone inside except for the sound of my own internal voice.

Programming is a very lonely way of life. It was not until much later in my role as a trainer that I came to realise that the six year old I mentioned earlier and

I were actually intrinsically linked. Due to our initiations and programming, she and I had become a conduit to facilitate our death due to end time programming. She was to engage in shut-down programming processes, which in turn triggered me into carrying out the deed of killing the body. This felt like a death sentence, which like the sword of Damocles' could drop at any time without us knowing. This was the point that I knew I had to try and free myself of the programming curse that had been put on me.

It was at this point that another sixteen-year-old protector came into the body to take us from the family home and put us in a hostel for nine young people. I did not know where I was at the time, but I did feel that maybe I was finally safe away from the coven. During this time however, I was out of where we were living and encountered the father, another Satanist, on his motorbike, and he was following me. This caused the onset of accessing, which was a worse form of contact with the coven than ever. Accessing is when the coven meet or telephone you, access a vulnerable alter using hypnosis, and take them with you, back to the coven setting. This was the first time, and was one of the worst accessings that I have ever experienced. I was called upon to show my loyalty to the coven by 'assisting' in another coven sacrifice, only this time it was not one of our own children. This 'assistance' I was again hypnotised into doing was forced upon me after being beaten into submission, literally. This was the point I experienced my first encounter with the omega programming as I had an overwhelming desire to kill the body. I even attempted suicide on autopilot, only to be mistaken for being an attention seeker by a hospital who, to be fair, knew nothing of my programming or what I had been through.

For many years, I was accessed and was used as a trainer to punish me for deserting the coven. The coven leaders knew I did not have any desire for carrying out my role anymore, so they took great delight in making me do it. They always made me start programming children too, preferably for them, as young as possible, to remind me not be insubordinate with them. As for me, I got more and more depressed knowing what was happening to innocent victims at my hands. I experienced regular torture too during that time, such as having needles put under my fingernails as a reminder of what would happen to me if I were to leave the coven. I felt trapped, like I would never be able to get away from the rapists of my life.

The final straw for me was being programmed and then raped by an older male, for which I was then, in a double bind, named a rapist myself. I had already been told that I was not a proper man because the coven had removed my male genitalia  due to my being a bad person, and I believed them so much that I was terribly ashamed of myself for this, and so a male on male sexual rape was my ultimate degradation. I felt violated and disgusted with myself, and when I was told that I was to programme this man who had raped me, I could take no more. I did their bidding, but I then ran away to try and tell the police, but ended up somewhere I did not know, and was then admitted into a psychiatric unit, but not understanding why; I was totally confused.

During my stay on the psychiatric unit I was given leave time access the shops in the city. Unbeknownst to me however, someone I knew had told the coven leaders where we were and I was accessed in the nearby hospital car park every time I was given my afternoon leave. You see, the hospital did not understand my programming, let alone the DID, so they did not take what I was saying seriously.

When the coven picked me up they put me in a car and I lost time, and I could not get away from them because I am in a wheelchair and cannot walk. Here I was reprogrammed. They programmed me into acting like everything was normal, a little bit like the screen alters we used to have in the system, but even though I knew they were making me lie about my abuse and my position in the coven, my mouth told a different story, and I found myself discrediting myself to the health professionals around me. Following my stay in hospital, however, I was sent back to where I was living before, and the daily accessing started happening again.

Over the years I was reprogrammed a number of times, and I was also reprogrammed to mind control other people again. New people were ‘persuaded’ to join the ‘coven family’, mostly homeless people with no family looking for lasting attachments, and I was the first person shoved forward to hypnotise and access them. I will always remember the mental health problems a homeless teenager had, and the disturbances and psychosis that ensued as a result of her programming that I ‘assisted’ in. I will never forgive myself for the part I had to play in that.

Things came to a head when we were being accessed in our own flat, without a soul, let alone the police, ever finding out. They would arrive at the flat stating that they were debt collectors, admit themselves into my home, and since we were having money issues anyway, this was quite a regular occurrence. From there they would either rape us in situ, or just take us to a wood-panelled house where rituals took place and start using us as ‘normal’ again. There I learnt, in a deep and complete manner, how to programme people alone, mainly children and teenagers, into a full state of omega programming, whereas before I was always assisted as I was not fully trusted. Although being horse whipped first to remind me of my place, I began to do my role. Omega programming or suicide programming comes from Greenbaum programming, and I was taught to use hypnosis to great effect. The one problem was that they expected me to be psychopathic, not caring about anyone, but I did. I felt increasingly guilty at what I was doing and came home sobbing. I felt my life was worthless because I had, albeit in a forced manner due to mind control, done to innocents what had been done to me, and I felt my death was the only answer. The double bind in this situation, though, was that the coven had put a failsafe into my programming, so that if ever I wanted to leave the coven then a programme would be started by Sybil, who has an internal omega switch, which would make me end our time forever.

It was a little later that we were rescued by Dr Pat Frankish and moved to a safe place, where the coven could never find us. We have support now 24/7, so we are kept safe from our mind control, but also from the coven who seek to kill us for leaving them. It has been a tumultuous time for me as I could not cope with the intense guilt from the cold and clinical programmed life that I had experienced since my body age of fifteen years old. I have not even told and processed much of what I have written here in therapy yet, as it is so hard to face what I have been made to do. Why I write it here though, is to warn people that even dabbling with mind control is a dangerous affair and can cost people their lives.

I now have a timebomb ticking inside me: my omega, end time or suicide programming, and I don't know how to de-programme myself. This is because I and others in my system had so much experimental programming laid down inside our DID system that we do not know if we are on our head or our heels, so to speak.

Others inside still see me as a coven trainer and master programmer, and Celestine as the high priestess of their coven, and as such they still look to me to re-programme them. This is a bitter pill to swallow, and I hate it. Also, the six-year-old alter and I are linked as we have become a conduit to those trying to keep us constantly in a state of end time programming. Many have come out since becoming safe for the first time ever, and have also used me personally as a conduit to write down features of programming that have been used on our system. It is only now, however, that I understand why they engage with me in this manner. The system is shifting more and more towards end-time programming now we are in a safe space as there is no one to update our programming. It is an ever-growing programme that adapts itself to current times in an effort to end our time on earth.

If there is one thing I could say about programming, it is that it makes a mockery of life. It seeps into your soul and damages everything, every sinew of your whole being, and you can't get your life back. I know that I have a long way to go before I heal, and I doubt that I ever actually will, fully. All I know is that I will never be safe if I am alone, and I need support to maintain a meaningful life. It is only through this that I have a chance of getting a degree of my life back.

# Chapter 7: More inside stories

## Various alters

The medium of television was used as part of our programming from when the body was around 10 or 11 years old. Because we are such visual learners, this was honed and used by the programmers to maximum effect. Bearing this in mind, I am going to try to help you understand a little of how this was done, as a combination of what would be called today 'social learning theory' and visualisation and terror in the form of psychic surgery. This was used, to my belief, with the greatest of effect.

My subsystems, in part, are aware of the scene in 'Star Trek, The Next Generation', which was used in the Nemesis Borg programming. Contained within the specified scene is a point where the Borg Queen's head, brain and spinal cord are lowered down into a 'host' body. She has a collection of 'pipes', coming from her head, from which she communicates to drones and many systems of space ships within the Borg culture. They all follow her voice and do her bidding, and she controls the movements and everything the Borg spheres do.

What does this mean for us? The body's father attempted to programme an internal version of the Borg Queen by transplanting a physical representation of her into our system, in the form of Vera the high priestess, also the gassing lady. She seems to be higher up in the hierarchy of our system than most, and a design was implemented for her to take the high priestess-ship when Vera finally retired from her position within the coven.

The representation of Vera was designed to lead and teach other covens with the underground circuit community, thus controlling them too, as the television show depicted. So far, she has remained mainly inactive, but there is an increasing chance of her making an attempt to take over. For some time now, there have been references to our lives being 'crashed' or killed inside the system, and Vera is designed to be the ultimate 'car crasher'. She has a duty to fulfill her leadership role and wishes to go underground to any coven she knows of whom will accept her, otherwise her role is to drive the system mad to the point of suicide.

Now is the time, for us to fight the Nemesis Borg Queen!

Paul of the Chorus

I am Satan. I am he. The one this is all about. Worship me. Satanic worship is worship of me. For I am Satan, or at least the internal one anyway. I guess you could say that you should fear me, because I am high up the pecking order in this DID system. I guess you could say I was put here via forced dissociation, but I am here and am not going anywhere.

I don't acknowledge trauma. Everything that happened to me I chalk up to experience, and take it that one day when I die, it will make me a god, like my 3D counterpart. I have taken part in necromancy, which was unpleasant but hey, it all serves to show me that I am important. I was created to be important in our system. I took part in pain contests against other alters and I won so here I am. A pain contest pits alters against each other when they are tortured by the coven. It's what got me where I am. The more pain you can handle the better, and I won. So I am important.

I am ageless. That means as a spirit being I never get any older. I was raped by men all the time, but as a spirit being you feel nothing because you are in the upper realms. You only see it happening from very high up in the air. When I am given the chance, which is not very often, I try to invoke the 3D Satan to help me. To help me kill the body because that is part of my job. I was always taught that death was my ultimate victory, as death is the culmination of everything I have worked for.

Other alters don't have to listen to anything I say, but they do because they fear me. And I was taught to make them fear me more, by holding internal pain contests using the trauma others experienced in the past. I can make alters spin with pain and make them beg for me to stop. I can recall what you would call traumas, but they only serve to show me how to do my job for the coven better.

I am a fighter. I have talked in therapy before, but I don't like doing so. There is an unspoken rule among those of us in the upper echelons that you don't break the code of silence put there by the master himself, and I follow it to the letter and made a pact. I cut my arms and joined the master in our blood, becoming one to prove my loyalty. I have done things that would make your blood curdle. The master told me to be loyal and I would be sent to the spirit realm early if I did not do it. I have had to eat the flesh of the body's own baby, and drink the blood, which again was unpleasant but hey, that is what comes with making a pact of loyalty.

If I admitted to experiencing trauma it would be a weakness. I am strong like Aleister Crowley and Anton Lavey. They are who I model myself on. They were loyal.

Here endeth my narrative.

Satan

I am fifteen years old and I am a breeder. A breeder is someone who makes babies for the coven to then take their lives. I was programmed at 15 years old to be a breeder. My son was conceived at a coven ritual on 7 September. The 'marriage to the beast ritual' happens every year, like clockwork, since a six-year-old alter was first initiated, and involves the consummation of the marriage. This is not done by one male in the coven, but rather all of them, having sex with you one after another. They call it Satanic Revels, but really I just felt like a dirty whore and I still do.

Being pregnant whilst knowing your baby will be murdered is a strange and horrid thing. It all feels surreal. Dissociation and programming teaches you to be cold, clinical and unfeeling about it; but I couldn't be. Being a new alter, I did not at first know I was pregnant but when I found out I was, I loved him from the moment I knew he was in my tummy. This is where the programming kind of went wrong with me. I wasn't some automaton with no feelings. I loved this child of mine and was determined to get away from the coven with him.

Oh, how I tried to get away from the coven. I felt an affinity and bond to this child inside me and I tried to run away a few times, only to be dragged back kicking and screaming. I was beaten afterwards and I wondered whether my baby would survive anyway. I even jumped out of a bedroom window, but all to no avail and it made me ashamed of myself.

As my pregnancy went on the master programmer tried to distance me from my child using programming, but my bond of love, I believe, was already too strong. Yes, I spent a lot of the time terrified and heavily dissociated in turn afterwards, but it didn't truly work.

The programmers kept me locked in a dirty grey room with dirty sheets on the bed in preparation for delivery. I expected to have my baby full term, as they told me it would take nine months to have him, but the coven decided they wanted my little man to come into the world on Good Friday, just over six months after my baby's conception. They put an injection and needle in my arm, and they used something that looked like a crochet hook to break my waters, and these things brought my labour on.

A number of hours after this happened my son, Matthew, came into the world. He came in with much pain, and I got a tear in my woman's nether regions, but it was the best pain I ever had because I loved him. When I heard his crying it was really high pitched and they laid him on my belly for a very short time, and he looked really red. I was crying too, but when they took him away from me it was the worst thing ever to happen to me. I tried to get to him then, but my body was too much like jelly, and I was too weak to run so I couldn't. This is one thing I will forever feel guilty for though.

The worst part of the ritual was hearing my little man Matthew crying, and then hearing the crying stop, and knowing that they had taken his life. That is the last thing I really remember, as someone else came along because I dissociated badly. But hearing the crying stop was the worst pain ever. That traumatised me the most, I think. No amount of hypnosis that they did to me afterwards took away the trauma, and they tried so hard to make me forget but they couldn't get it to work properly. Sure I was foggy, but it was still there. I can only put it down to the fact that I loved Matthew too much.

Now I feel bereft. As I write, it is just after Easter and the pain of my loss doesn't go anywhere. I feel hate at the people that tried to make me forget and be like an automaton, and that will never go away. Being pregnant at 15 is hard, but to have my baby killed just for the sake of a coven ritual is something I will NEVER EVER forget, or forgive. I can't.

Sara

# Chapter 8: Therapy from the inside

## Carrie Anne Smith and alters

> *"We are the Chorus. We are a group of alters mainly without names, and as such we flow freely when we talk, to teach and explain, with much fluidity. We reside deep inside our system and only came out about a year ago. Life with mind control is hard, but there is a way through it. It's all about learning to connect again, to touch base and become as one, even though there are many thousands of us inside. We came to bring light to a darkened path, and promote healing in therapy. That is the way forward."*
>
> The Chorus

I, the host of our Dissociative Identity Disorder (DID) system, came to know of the Chorus about a year ago, and boy did they give me a shock! They arrived into the conscious realm at a very dark time, when one of our protectors was being used as a scribe for dark ones inside to communicate information about mind control programming to our psychologist. The Chorus were led by one of their only alters with a name, Paul, who was originally taught a lot about programming by listening to the coven himself, and to help in therapy he immediately started to write programming 101 guides to teach our psychologist more about our system and the extent of its mind control. This was very scary to begin with, as all of a sudden 1,843 alters came flooding into our system, all purporting to be from the light side, and all expecting me, their host, to trust them. Like any new alter, I initially viewed them with caution, but over time they proved to be more than trustworthy, in fact teaching me just how complex the many thousands of alters in our system there actually were.

The Chorus also came to help the Psychic Surgeon in our system speak out against what was happening to him. This alter was taught to perform Satanist psychic surgery. He was claimed by the coven itself to teach and take part in psychic surgery, and maim people using hypnosis, and post-hypnotic inductions for life. In our internal landscape he also had a surgical team who helped him to take people into very deep hypnotic states by using a form of 'hypnotic anaesthetic', but at this stage they were turning against the Psychic Surgeon.

> *"I was trying to write our post-hypnotic inductions for therapy, to prove my existence and indeed what we went through, but the surgery team did not want this, for they were still on the dark side. I write without blinking to help me stay awake, but they were counter-hypnotising me, with my very own inductions. So, until the Chorus came along I had no protection over them, so I just used to go into a deep state of somnambulism (hypnosis) myself when writing, along with*

*the host, and others in our system. This was when the Chorus came and helped me. I can safely write and show how different alters in the system lost bodily functions, because of them."*

The Psychic Surgeon

This freeing up of the Psychic Surgeon by the Chorus helped a lot of our alters to start talking about their true stories in therapy.

*"Hi. I'm Celestine and I'm a girl. I don't reveal my age because that would be very dangerous for me. People in the coven don't like young people in their upper echelons because it usurps their authority. They also think girls aren't important enough to bother about, so I stay quiet so they think I'm older than I actually am.*

*I was a regular girl, keeping myself to myself. I used to be quiet and loved to play board games. I used to sneak out into the body when no one was around because I didn't like all the sex stuff they [the coven] were doing to me. Men are nasty idiots when it comes to sex, and the coven liked regular orgies. That's what I hated.*

*The day they found me they dragged me out of the system when I just wanted to be inside. They had seen the way I could relax punters if I had to, so they thought I would be good for a specific job in the coven and they said it was a big responsibility. That's because I would be an example to women and girls in the coven... and I would come to learn how to do hypnosis, which they made out to be cool.*

*I didn't want a job like that because I don't like to be noticed. I did think though that it might stop the sex stuff that kept happening so I agreed to do what they wanted me to do.*

*The first time I was hypnotised it was really weird. It was like this. Two people were speaking different stuff in both ears, and I started to feel sleepy. I remember one of them saying that I was surrounded in a golden light and to let my wrist rise up when the balloon tied to it did. I assume this happened as they counted down from ten and I don't remember too much else. I was aware, though, that I nearly died during hypnosis but they rescued me which I didn't really believe.*

*After several similar times of hypnosis, they said I was ready to begin training to be the new gassing lady like Vera. Vera was the high priestess, and was a scary person. I didn't like her and wanted to hide, but they pushed me into the limelight and some coven folk didn't like it. They beat me up when no one was around because they said some people thought they were better than me.*

*Then the training began big time. I was taught hypnotic inductions and how to take people into a deep state of hypnosis. They liked me doing it because they said I was super calm, but really I was what I think they call dissociated all the time and that was how I handled it. I was also taught how to give hypnotic general anaesthetics to put people in a really deep sleep – the person inside who I was learning with and who was to be the coven boss in training wasn't as good at putting people to sleep as me, they said.*

> *As an anaesthetic person, like Vera before me, I also learnt to be part of a surgery team who helped with psychic surgery. They said I would be good with the kids in the coven as I could relax them good but I didn't want to do that so I said no, that I just wanted to be a normal kid. They then beat me up and raped me and made me spin out the room and I never did it again. I knew I had no choice in what I had to do.*
>
> *Let's be clear about one thing. Spinning is programming and it's horrid. It leaves you feeling not in charge of your own head. They weren't over bad with me when I did what they wanted me to do but woe betide me if I didn't. Us kids develop a resilience to abuse but you can't do that with programming. It knocks you for six before you have a chance to say Jack Robinson.*
>
> *I felt way guilty for putting people into trance states but, coward as I am, I was scared I would end up dead if I didn't do it. As high priestess I knew the messe noir, the 'black mass', but I hated it too. I knew the chants, but to me hypnosis done in a calm sing-songy voice to start with seemed like chanting too. And I hated the title 'gassing lady' because it made me sound like Vera.*
>
> *No kid should have gone through what I did. Now that I know we were to be a one system coven head, I hate the thought of it. Kids like me and Alistair should have been left to be kids. I didn't want to hypnotise people but I had no choice. And for that I will never forgive myself for. Programming kills. Think about it."*
>
> Celestine

At this time a number of alters came out and admitted that they were sex kittens. Beta sex kittens came about as a result of Greenbaum programming and were mind controlled into sex working (prostitution), pornography, and taking part in sexual cult rituals, to name but a few of their many roles (see chapter 2). Although they had been working in therapy for quite some time, many of them had not had the confidence to speak up and actually admit what their role was within our system. It had also brought much shame for them, which, up until that point they were unwilling to address.

> *"I guess you could say that I am a little stormy, but I am a sex kitten. I never used to admit it to anyone, let alone myself. As a sixteen year old with an attitude I was so ashamed of myself. It took me realising that I had been programmed into this stuff to realise it might not be my fault. I'm still working on believing that one, but I'm getting there. Programming stinks, but it takes learning to realise that this is all you know, and that you heal, change and grow."*
>
> A sex kitten

Sex kittens were programmed to enjoy the sexual acts that they were taking part in, so that their punters would pay the maximum amount. The fact that inside their own minds they would have found those experiences terrifying was immaterial. The programming they had undergone made up for this. For us now it can be summed up by the song from Miss Saigon (Schonberg & Boublil,

1989) in which one of the characters, a prostitute sings, 'The movie in my mind, the dream they leave behind, a scene I can't erase', for us the programming is the movie in our alter's minds, but the scene left behind their programming is something they cannot erase because of the trauma that they experienced. This can be summed up by the words of one of our 12-year-old sex kittens:

> *"Now I remember that I was programmed to please the punters I feel sick. When you are under the influence of programming everything is like it's not happening and is surreal... but when you go into therapy everything becomes real and it's horrid to start with... until you process it all."*
>
> A 12-year-old sex kitten

For many of these sex kittens, the trauma and pain was further compounded by the fact that one of their roles was to be a breeder – a person or alter who is used by the coven to get pregnant so that the coven can use her baby as a sacrifice. For those of us who were breeders it was one of the most traumatic things we had to go through. As well as the trauma that is involved in a ritual such as this, there is the physical pain, but most of all there is the grief at the taking of your baby's life. For us, the only way to take the long road to healing was to start by talking it all through in therapy. This had to come from us as it is one of the hardest things to admit to. The next stage in our healing was that we all agreed inside that we wanted a church service to say goodbye to our babies. Our therapist helped us to do achieve this and to get through it, and we even had a wake of sorts. We invited a few trusted people and it meant a lot to us that they were there. This assisted therapy from the inside, as we all had a shared grief which we could work through and support each other together, and that was very important.

> *"If we had not got each other, I don't think I would have lived to tell the tale. Without the help of everyone inside, I would surely have committed suicide from the pain of losing my baby."*
>
> Carrie Anne Smith

> *"Time passes for us breeders, but after what happened things will never be the same again. The fact that we were programmed to allow this to happen and, with clinical coldness, was wiped when we started talking about the death of our babies in therapy. It is something that, now we know what happened, we will never forgive ourselves for. The fact that it is not safe to go back to the resting places of our babies for us, hurts like heck too. We said goodbye, but that will never be enough. All we have now are the memories, and those memories will never be enough for us. All we can do is stay united in grief, and work through it all together."*
>
> The sex kitten collective

Supporting each other from the inside about our babies is as important as it is with our ritual abuse history. In the Satanist setting, there were many annual ritual days which all had a profound effect on many of us within the system. Many of them, like the 'Marriage to the Beast' ritual as mentioned previously, were consummated with sexual relations every year, and orgies would ensue as a result of these 'satanist revels' (sexual rituals). The fact that these happened every year meant that a large number of our alters, mostly females, were involved in them. It is only now that we are realising that we need to work as a collective to heal from them. The problem is that within our system we do not have the level of co-consciousness required to speak to each other (being able to have a mutual conversation) about what is happening. This can only be done by speaking out and hoping that someone inside hears you. By having someone there to listen we can go forward together, and work on creating a shared storyline which we can then begin to heal from.

## References

Schonberg CM and Boublil A, 1989.

# Chapter 9: Working with support staff

## Carrie Anne Smith and alters

Having a good support system is vital to a Dissociative Identity Disorder (DID) system with a history of mind programming. Without this it can become impossible for the survivors of the system to ever be able to live a meaningful life that is healing – filled. Indeed, for people without DID support systems can be important, for example influencing general mental health and important life decisions, but for many survivors of ritual abuse with co-morbidities of DID and mind programming, family and 'friends' can be very unsafe as they were or are involved within the coven. It is only through establishing a totally safe and new support system that these survivors can begin to heal.

At the heart of a support network for complex DID systems is the therapist or psychologist. He or she needs to believe what may sometimes seem impossible because of the heinous incidences that occur at the hands of the ritual abusers. This professional also needs to be able to educate and train support staff about what works with his or her clients, whilst applying attachment-based therapy to the people with DID. This complex support network can also encompass outside agencies such as NHS psychiatrists or social workers, but for the purposes of this chapter we will concentrate on support staff and the important role they play in creating a hope of healing for their client.

> *"Having a support system of support workers for us has been and continues to be vital. Most importantly, they keep us safe from harm, but the therapeutic attachments that I, and indeed all of us, have established with them is a lifeline. They help us look after our inside children and have a laugh and a joke with the teenagers, whilst all of the time providing a stable emotional base for us all to work in therapy."*
>
> Lioness Kayleigh and Claire

> *"For our system, we moved into a new safe space with a totally new support system. We were not good at trusting people after our ritual abuse so this proved to be scary and also a challenge, as these people were hand-picked by the psychologist we trusted to a degree at that stage, and we had to get used to them. We had a small team of people, totalling four in number, and these individuals accompanied us everywhere except for when we went to bed. Gradually, as we met them all, we began to realise that they were safe people who we could maybe trust. This was not without its hiccups though, as many of our teenaged alters felt they did not need anyone, and being kept safe when they wanted to be back with the coven which they perceived to be 'safe', was a constant source of concern for our support staff."*
>
> Sara

Support staff involved with this DID system were hand-picked to work in their service. It is always important to make sure that support staff are a good fit, as if not, they may doubt or even disbelieve their clients. Also, staff may not be able to connect with so many dissociative identities, so people who have an open mind, even to a new and unknown condition, are vital. A willingness to learn is also important, because DID incorporates so many different inside people that there may be a number of different interests within the collective, so an ability to think on your feet when switching occurs is a must. Finally, the notion of safety and being as safe as possible is something that needs to be positively reinforced, because it can be hard for a system, that has never been in this position to believe that they are safe.

There were a number of approaches that the support staff needed to conquer in order to work successfully with everyone who presented themselves. For a start, every time a young child came into the open, they needed to be looked after in an age-appropriate way. Support staff had to learn to speak to a child in an adult body, in the way, for example, that you would speak to a three or five year old. This also meant they needed support with being kept safe from hot items in the kitchen, helped with their finances as they did not understand it at all, and be helped to look after themselves by taking needed medication, to name just a few things. Support staff were also needed to help the small inside children to learn to play, as due to their abuse they had not learned to do so. For us, we found that working with our little insiders in an age-appropriate way was vital in assisting with their beginning to heal.

As the reader may be aware, DID systems can be very large, and at this stage it became apparent that the support staff were meeting very large numbers of alters, and that this was a lot of information about them all to remember. The senior support worker wondered how to combat this issue until she came upon a way of assisting staff to learn about these individuals. Record cards were obtained, and her and the host of the DID system wrote together a card about each inside person that came out, with their name, age and basic information about them. This greatly assisted support staff to learn as they worked and come to recognise that each alter was and is an individual.

These individuals within such a large DID system were also light or innocent and traumatised, or dark, which means they were coven loyal and sometimes were perpetrators to other alters or other people within the coven or beyond. Dark alters were not to be trusted unless they came to the light side, and as such wanted to go back to the coven and tried to on many various occasions. It therefore became apparent to support staff that they needed to watch dark alters like a hawk, as they would try to harm the body given half a chance, or worse, try to abscond back to the coven. Establishing where dark alters are located within the system and their role is important for support staff, as then any ambush can be anticipated and prevented, if the need arises.

With the presence of dark alters within the system, a need arose for support workers to watch who was around when the system went out anywhere, as the wish to go back to the coven for a number of inside people was very intense indeed. With this in mind, forms were produced to monitor who was seen around the outside environment, with a mind to collating them to see if the coven continued to follow this DID system e.g. when on public transport. The form, which was produced by the then senior support worker of the system's service, required support workers to detail dates, times and where the person was seen along with details of what they looked like. This also assisted in calming down the whole system, as they felt that they were heard, whilst assisted in looking for patterns in the appearances of any potential abusers. It also brought the clients and support workers to a better understanding of safety and what could potentially happen.

> *"At this point in time, we became very unwell, nearly psychotic in fact, believing we had to get to safety with our psychologist, as we believed flashbacks of abusers getting into our home was in the here and now. We also, because of the end time suicide programming, were giving away our property in the belief it was the best thing to do. We were ruled by dark alters reprogramming us from inside, and as a result of support staff not getting or understanding the situation at hand, morale became very low as they struggled to cope with the onslaught of mind control programming that was going on inside our system."*
>
> Storm, Charisma and Cathartic

This was the darkest time the system had experienced since arriving in their new environment. Due to the low morale within the staff at this time, a new and much larger support staff team was established with the inclusion of males, and people who had absolutely no understanding of DID whatsoever. For the staff, shorter and fewer hours with a 13 strong team allowed them to get regular breaks from the system, but what it meant for the system was a very unsafe time, as they struggled to come to terms with males and inappropriate staff who did not want to understand came into the service.

It cannot be stressed enough that the larger team was given to this DID system as a result of the staff feeling safer, however for the system it was a very dark time, and the general consensus among these survivors is that a small team is much better and psychologically safer for all concerned. When there are too many staff in a team, there is no continuity of care in real time, and with staff morale being at a low, aggression was a regular feature of both staff and clients' communication. It was the blackest of black times, and in retrospect the system can see why the team became larger, but they would still like to warn people that if at all possible a smaller team will always foster greater trust and a much warmer outlook and therapeutic attachment, than a larger one.

> *"If we could say one thing about what happened, we understand why we ended up with a big team, but a smaller one is much better for us to feel safer and be able to talk more freely and trusting with staff. Without that it is 2 scary 4 words."*
>
> Claire and Nicky

For the emotional welfare of staff, it should be pointed out that if psychological support is offered to the support workers, and they are helped to understand what is going on in relation to their feelings about the system, this can be nothing except productive. Through the use of group sessions to educate supporters, and one-to-one sessions to help them come to terms with the impact of what has been happening for the system, the support staff can better work with the survivors and morale among all concerned can potentially be increased so that staff and clients alike are working together more.

Eventually, this is what happened for the aforementioned system. As the programming re-stabilised so did the system, and they came to realise the impact of what had happened for both them and their staff. Due to the nature of DID, and with the inclusion of dark alters within the system, many of the lighter one's did not remember what they had been told, and it shocked them when they were told what had happened. This is something that is important for any system to know, as knowledge about those inside alerts them into foreseeing when problems are up and incoming, and knowledge is always an advantageous way of fighting the darkness. It is uncomfortable for any alter to hear, but the pros far outweigh the cons.

During the dark times there was little or no trust between the system and its staff, and this was a very negative culmination of what happened. As things calmed down again, however, and trust began to return between the support staff and the survivors. Trust has since been key to alters feeling comfortable enough to disclose some of the darker secrets of the system's abuse. It may be useful to note, for any system of survivors that trust has its foundations in belief in the truth of the system's abuse, even when what has happened seems somewhat far-fetched. This helps the support system to grow in confidence, and in turn assists the system with being able to deepen the work that is done in psychology sessions. Without this, dark alters can get a foothold in the door and try to abscond, or even change a system's programming which is very much to the detriment of the clients concerned.

> *"One thing that shocked us the most was the knowledge that while the programming may be better some days than others, it would always be there. It's like how can it never go away? It rocks your world and it rocks your confidence in yourselves... there is a grieving process to go through to acknowledge the fact that your whole world will never be the same as other people's... and the worst bit about it is knowing that there is programming that could cause your own suicide when you least expect it. It is an excruciating pain that never goes away."*
>
> Sara and Izzie

This information should help support staff to understand why their role in keeping their system safe is so important, and that trust between the insiders and the supporters is vital in keeping a system safe. Whilst programming is something best left for therapy sessions as it is so complex in nature, it is important that supporters achieve a basic understanding of how lethal programming can be if left to get into a state of crisis, as it can literally be a matter of life and death if a system is left with no support system. An understanding of the grief that a system goes through when the survivors come to acknowledge that the programming is there for life is also important. The German word 'Verstehen' means in essence empathetic understanding, and with careful education from psychology support, it can be possible for the support staff to empathetically understand and relate to the place that the system finds themselves in. It is at this point that support staff and clients can begin to discover the heinous activities that Satanist individuals are actually capable of.

Programming, at its core, is an act of pure evil and it takes many forms, from the use of Greenbaum programming, to hypnosis, to the application of behavioural psychology in a negative way, to name but a few. These forms of mind control tear the system apart, and it is important to combat the after effects of programming with things that are age appropriate and normal for any child or teenager to do. This helps alters to have the childhood that they never had due to mind control.

> *"When we came to our safe place, someone who assisted in getting us safe recommended that we have a playroom. This was a safe place we could all play and do arts and crafts or even play board games. It was a place for teens to hang out, the kids to play with dollies, and us tweenies who are in between to do our makeup and just have a normal childhood."*
>
> Katie

The creation of a normal childhood safe space is an important therapeutic intervention for all ages within a system, and indeed continues to be important to the healing of this system as a whole. In considering support staff's role in this place of play, it is useful to understand that each individual needs to be approached in an age-appropriate manner, or otherwise the little children in the system may not understand what has been said, and may become confused or scared because they don't 'get it'. Toys and books need to be focused on different ages, with support staff supporting the fun by playing with the child, 'tween' or teen at their age and level. If this play starts taking turns into re-enactment of the abuse, the supporter's role then changes to stirring memories of how they were distracted during past abuse, so play is more centred on fun than the actual dialogues that need to be broached in therapy.

Along with therapeutic play comes support with the serious everyday activities of daily living, such as doing the washing, personal care, and most of all the paying of household bills, to name but three examples. Using the example of this DID system, all three of these activities needed support and encouragement to carry them out, but household bills got severely neglected. Bills were not being paid to the point where on a cold day there was no central heating because the money had run out and debt collectors were beginning to become involved. Since this had happened before, there was a need for financial appointees to discuss these issues with the then host of the system, and then were appointed to look after the system's finances. This continues to be a useful arrangement, and support staff can assist too, in that they can see that personal money given to their clients is spent on food, cleaning materials and toiletries, before it is spent on toys, games and craft items. It is not for staff to play a controlling role, but rather an advisory role which is nevertheless persuasive and firm.

# Section 3: Therapeutic approaches

This section considers the theoretical underpinnings of different approaches to therapy, and how the therapist needs to look after themselves whilst engaging in therapy with mind-programmed people. It also describes of training for support staff.

# Chapter 10: Attachment and trauma informed care in the therapy of dissociative individuals

Pat Frankish

The very existence of Dissociative Identity Disorder (DID) means that the primary processes of developing an integrated social identity have failed or been interrupted. Sometimes this is by design and sometimes by accident, and sometimes a mix of both. It is useful to consider the different theories and relate them to the presentation, the way a specific DID system is. This chapter will look at the writings of Winnicott, Bowlby, Klein and Mahler, and relate them to the condition of DID. No two people who are made up of a collection of alters to make a workable system will be the same, so these are ideas to use as a basis of understanding.

## Winnicott

Donald Winnicott in his seminal work *The Child, the Family and the Outside World*, described the processes of early childhood that lead to the healthy development of a sense of self as a whole, integrated being. He also described what can happen if the optimal environment is not there for the developing child. He considered the beginning of life to be crucial and he spoke about the power of maternal preoccupation in setting the child on a healthy route to a good outcome. Maternal preoccupation is the state in which a mother can think of nothing else other than her baby and is fully preoccupied with its needs and what it is experiencing. Winnicott stated that only the biological mother can provide this but that if a substitute is required, there can still be a good outcome, albeit a different one. Of course, this is not something that can be tested scientifically for an individual child, but we do have evidence that a good early start has positive effects. The building blocks for personality development are there in that first relationship.

The child who is born into a ritualistic cult, especially if bred for a cult, is at risk, straight away, of not fulfilling its potential. If the baby is not reared by its biological mother, as may well be the case, there will potentially be an emotionally traumatic response and, if the baby is born to be used in the cult, it will be deliberately prevented from developing a whole personality.

This begins at birth and explains the interference in the natural process of personality development which leads to DID.

The next stages of development, bearing in mind that this client group are already on a damaging trajectory, involves the integration into the family. In optimal development the mother is the main attachment figure, with the father or another adult, supporting the mother in the role of second attachment figure. If all goes well the child internalises both relationships and begins to grow into a person who can discriminate between people, trust and relate to more people, while developing their own unique personality. The child born into a cult will have this process deliberately disrupted so as to remove all trust and raise anxiety, leading to dependence on the cult for everything, including day-to-day survival. If deliberate dissociation is practiced, it will develop here with different personalities being required for different relationships and actions. For example, one cult figure will behave as if they value the child, another with hatred, another with physical pain, and so on. The child learns to be, or becomes, different when in the presence of each adult, and these different selves become fixed. In addition to those that are forced on the child, there will be some survival selves that grow from the natural part of the child. This is a complex process and explains why it is so hard to help people to understand the condition of DID.

Winnicott refers to the Outside World as the next stage the child needs to circumnavigate. Ideally a child needs to be able to relate to the outside world before attending school. The child in an ordinary home and family will gradually accommodate more people into its world, more ways of seeing and accepting differences and become more relaxed with their ability to discriminate and function. This provides the pathway to developing relationships in school and the wider world. A child who has had their ability to relate to others distorted by abuse and rituals, will struggle to go to school. What usually happens is that an alter develops that becomes 'the one who does school' and functions in that setting. The intellect is usually available to that alter and successful transition through school can happen. Because the alternative personality is complete for that function, others, like teachers and support workers, are not aware that the child has other alters for other functions. And the child who has been fully dissociated is not aware either that there are others inside, but will gradually become aware of lost time. Lost time is what happens when the personality switches to another and then switches back.

Within his many writings Winnicott talks about the impact of abuse and cruelty in childhood, including cruel parenting and neglect. He does not specifically say a lot about dissociation but it can be extrapolated from what he says about optimal development, that dissociation, particularly forced dissociation, will have permanent effects on the individual.

Using Winnicott to inform therapy would involve helping the different alters to identify themselves, value their identity and role in the whole personal system, recognise what happened to them, then help them to communicate with each other. The aim is to build a whole personality whilst valuing what each one contributes and leaving no-one out. There will be some who are very negative, maybe angry or suicidal, there will be others who have disabilities, and each will be carrying some part of the pain from early childhood. For the personality to be as fractured as it is in DID, it must start early, which is why looking at the early developmental theories is so useful.

## Bowlby

John Bowlby was working at about the same time as Winnicott. He is known as the father of attachment theory (see Chapter 2). It was Bowlby who first drew attention to the needs that children have for the presence of a safe adult who will meet their needs. Some of this work related to hospitalised children, where he observed that children separated from their parents went into a state of mourning and despair. He then studied more and arrived at his conclusions, which were written up in *The Secure Base*. It was originally called *The Making and Breaking of Affectional Bonds* in which he stresses the fact that children have to be able to make healthy attachments for them to be able later to make healthy detachments. Then, of course, more of both as they go through life.

Bowlby did not stress the need for the biological mother to be the attachment figure. He said that it is the person who is nearest (proximal) to whom the child will attach. The adult who is present and meets the needs in a warm and kind way will become the attachment figure and feature prominently in the development of the child's personality. It follows that the child who has the opportunity to form a strong and healthy attachment to a safe adult will have a good chance of growing up with a strong sense of self, with self-worth and the ability to make relationships.

Bowlby wrote about the consequences of not providing a 'Secure Base'; of not having a safe primary attachment figure. He described pathological mourning for those children who grew up feeling abandoned and unloved. He explains serious mental illness in relation to cruel parenting, neglectful parenting and inadequate parenting. Pathological mourning becomes severe depression, and physical attacks can lead to severe self-harm or aggression towards others. Inconsistent parenting leads to anxiety and so on. This theory would account for serious psychotic illnesses that follow when an individual never forms a whole self, or a coping group of selves.

For a child growing up in a cult there will be no reliable attachment figure. The main providers of physical attention may do this cruelly. Emotional support will be missing or deliberately inconsistent; one minute indicating love, and the next anger, so the child never knows what to expect. This cultivates the development of different personalities, with each one being present for the role that is defined for them. Some alters will stay as children while others develop to meet the changing demands of the next stages of life.

Using Bowlby's theory in therapy would involve making sure that the rules of therapy are strictly maintained. That is, a safe space at the time that is booked, for long enough to feel safe, and to continue for several years to enable a new growth processes to happen. It is not easy for all the alters to accept one therapist but it is  necessary if there is to be some integration of the selves into one, or at least to a point that they all recognise each other. For the therapist, it is like having group therapy and can be very demanding. Sessions need to be at least double sessions and sometimes more than once a week.

## Mahler

Mahler's research led to a description of behaviours that develop over the period from birth to the formation of a 'self'. She called it psychological birth. She tracked the stages of development that are passed as the process of forming an identity happens. From these descriptions it is possible to identify the stage at which an interruption in the process could have happened. This then links to age and the home circumstances at the time. To have a formed identity and to become a social being that can relate to other people, it is necessary to circumnavigate these stages. The young person who is brought up with deliberate destruction of the single identity cannot progress through these stages. What we find in DID, however, is that some personalities (alters) are at one stage and others at other stages. This is very confusing for support staff and others who relate to the person with DID. It's not possible to know from day to day, or even hour to hour, who is going to be present.

The stages she described have clear behavioural descriptions making them fairly easy to recognize once you know them. The first one, linked to very early emotional development from a few weeks to about 10 months, is called differentiation.

At this stage, behaviours are all self-referenced and the world is very small, consisting of the child's immediate surroundings. We see this stage in adults with profound disabilities, with catatonia, dementia and with severe autism. We also see them in people who have experienced trauma, where they withdraw from contact with the world, hiding under the duvet, unable to communicate. There is an earlier stage of symbiosis but this is very rarely seen in anyone other than a newborn. However, if trauma occurs at the newborn stage, there may be an alter who is at that stage.

The next stage, associated with the approximate ages of 10 to 15 months, is called 'practicing' and corresponds with that stage of rapid development where the child acquires lots of new skills. These are then practiced to competence and then added to the repertoire of behaviours that the child has. Practicing behaviours are very obvious in autism and other obsessive conditions where repetition and stuckness play a big part in the presentation. At this stage there is still very limited or no two-way interaction. The child is very dependent on the adult to lead and maintain all aspects of life. If trauma occurs during this stage the consequent adult will have fixed patterns of behavior that are very stuck, be quite unattached to people, and possibly engage in self-destructive behaviours. In other words, the self-referenced behaviours develop a wider repertoire.

After these early stages there is a move on to two-way interaction and the development of social skills. The next two stages are called early and then late rapprochement, and are all about developing and learning how to relate to others in two-way interaction, the beginnings of being sociable. This probably starts the day the child can say "no" or run away. The beginnings of challenge! The role of the adult is to be available and reliable as the child explores its own abilities and its impact on others, as well as learning to accommodate the effect of others' behaviour on them. A huge learning process, ideally moving from two-way games to negotiation and the acceptance of the needs of others. At the end of this process, around the age of three and a half if all goes well, there will be a rapprochement crisis, and the sense of self is established. If this happens successfully it will be the foundation personality for the rest of the life of that person.

Within a DID system, there may be some alters who have reached individuation and others stuck at other stages, making communication internally very difficult. The mature adult alters become responsible for keeping everyone safe. In systems where there are no adult alters there will be a different presentation with high risk of serious mental health diagnoses in addition to the DID diagnosis.

Mahler stressed the need for the presence of a significant other in order for the stages to be progressed through. If the significant other is cruel or inconsistent (or both) there will be a disturbance in the process. In DID there will be likely to be a range of different alters at all the different stages and each one will have associations or maybe memories of incidents that occurred in their abuse that led to them being stuck where they are.

## Klein

Melanie Klein was the first analyst who said that the influence on the development of the personality starts at or before birth. Most people had assumed, it seems, that babies and small children didn't start to become people until there were out of babyhood. Klein, like Winnicott and Bowlby, stressed the need for the available mother or mother substitute to be available and able to accept and process the full range of feelings that the baby experiences. She referred to babies as experiencing a murderous rage when their needs are not met, and they are powerless to meet their needs themselves. She talked about how adults who have not had their infantile needs met will have negative consequences of mental illness, anger and despair. She described the stages of development, going from the paranoid schizoid position of infancy to the resolution of the depressive position ideally by the age of three or four. This resolution comes from being able to accept good and bad in the same person and follows from the mother not meeting a need instantly. When the child can accept that the mother can let them down but still be a good person, they have reached that stage of maturity that will allow them to move on with their intellectual and social development.

It is clear from the above that there are many similarities between Winnicott's 'outside world' level, Bowlby's secure attachment, Mahler's psychological birth and Klein's resolution of the depressive position. They are all saying, in different ways, that a child grows a sense of self as a good and worthwhile person within the relationship with a safe and loving adult.

As has been mentioned above, it is possible to have alters at all stages of emotional and personality development within one physical person with DID. This means that they are very difficult to diagnose, treat and look after properly. As they will have some alters who are loyal to their abusers, they often need protection in order to survive. It's almost impossible to assess capacity as some alters have it and some do not. These issues will be explored more in other chapters. It's important here to recognize that some alters will have been traumatised before the stage of having any alters with a sense of self, and their behavior will reflect this.

## References

Bowlby J (1988) *A Secure Base*. London: Routledge.

Klein M (1945) *Love, Guilt and Reparation*. London: Vintage.

Mahler M Pine F and Bergman A (1979) *The Psychological Birth of the Human Infant*. New York: Basic.

Winnicott D W (1973) *The Child, the Family and the Outside World.* 2000. London: Penguin.

# Chapter 11: Resilience through complexity: a therapist's perspective

Pat Frankish

Helping someone therapeutically, and keeping going without being sucked into the trauma is a constant challenge for therapists working with mind control survivors. The aim of mind programming is to control. The person who has become trained by an experienced programmer, will have been trained to control, to some extent, the people they come in contact with. Their role is to make sure they are never discovered. Consequently, they are very skilled at being elusive, almost invisible, and always in control or seeking to be in control.

Having worked for some years with individuals who have been programmed by mind programming experts it has become clear to me that I, and others, have to find enough personal resources to both recognise and resist attempts to control me. From my perspective, and I think from other therapists' perspectives having spoken to a number of them, there is an element of survival, resilience and recovery. It has become clear to me over the years that full resolution of the mind control programming is probably not possible. Therapeutically, what we are aiming for is a level of tolerance which comes from understanding what cannot be changed. Programming that has been instigated from a very early age, i.e. pre-individuation, has become part of the person. This programming is embedded in the personality development. This is why attempting to 'remove it' can be seen as anti-therapeutic, because it removes part of the self. In practice that's not possible, as the core self of the mind-controlled person will switch to another alter when under threat.

One of the things that I noticed very early on in my therapeutic work with a mind programmed person, or system, was the way that I felt when I left the sessions – I usually left the session feeling very hungry. I reflected on the meaning of this and started to take food with me to eat on my way home in the car. It then became necessary, therapeutically, to analyse that reaction in myself. It was then that I realised that the trauma must belong to a very early stage of emotional development when food is an essential part of relationships between parents and children. Food is a primary necessity and anything that has spoiled the relationship around food will have been traumatic. It then led me on to think about why people would choose to mind control their children. And then to think about why any human being would choose to mind control any other human being. That line of thinking inevitably takes you to issues of control, and the knowledge that most people who seek control are those who have had no control. It is almost impossible to get to the primary cause. And it is impossible to get to the primary cause of most negative and destructive behaviour. We know that people who have become abusers were, I think without exception, abused themselves as children. But we also know that many people who were abused as children do not go on to become abusers. The question of why cults and covens and Satanist ritual abusers continue from one generation to the next is a difficult one. If we look back through history we can find stories, and pictures of human beings doing horrendous things to other human beings. Behaviour that is not seen in other animals. Some animals will kill and eat their own young if in a state of threat but there is no evidence of gratuitous harm to their own kind. So human beings are unusual in this and it is hard to accept.

Working with mind programming brings out feelings in the therapist that are fundamental to the human condition. Valerie Sinason, a leader in this field, in her book *Mental Handicap and the Human Condition*, captures significant elements of this thinking. The attitude of human beings to people who are perceived to be less than themselves is evident, painful and fundamental to the way that modern society operates. Prejudice against people who are intellectually disabled, disabled in other ways, have mental health difficulties, are from different ethnic origins and suchlike, is common. If we consider that all human beings have the potential to be controlled and made to do things that they wouldn't think to do themselves, then we can recognise the environment in which mind control abusers function.

There can be no doubt that some of the organisations exist to make money. Their victims are trained by mind control programming to perform for payment, usually offering sexual services, but can include anything for which payment can be collected. Victims are commodities; they are purely objects, and the can be discarded when no longer of value. Some of the people in therapy with mind control programming will have been exploited and harmed both physically and psychologically. I suspect that a significant number of them never get into therapy but become seriously mentally ill or die. The ones who do come into therapy are already survivors. This raises the question as to what enabled them to survive this far. The therapist needs to be alert to the strengths that are there, but also to the possibility of complex programming that is paradoxical. The individual may have been trained to present in a certain way that is meant to be the opposite of reality in order to put others, including therapists, off the scent. Over recent years there have been a number of organised groups that have been exposed for their exploitation of vulnerable people, male and female, particularly in the sex trade. Whether any of those groups have been exercising mind control programming has not come out into the public domain. Looking at these cases from a therapist's perspective I have wondered about the possibility that they are exercising physical control, perhaps using drugs, rather than mind control. And that is certainly easier. But I also think that if mind control was being used that most police officers and social workers who would be involved may not have knowledge of such a phenomenon. And as I said above it is hard to believe what people will do.

What has become evident to me in listening to a number of the people that I've worked with, is that there are groups who may be described as Satanist, who have rituals and celebrations with the full liturgy worshipping the devil in a similar way that Christians would worship God. These groups are different, often familial, and very secret. The children born into these groups are bred to become breeders to produce babies for sacrifice. This is a very difficult concept to accept but if the therapist can't accept it as a possibility, they are not in a very strong position to help the client that they're working with. In these cults they are trained from a very young age to be one person on the outside to go to school and appear normal. Then they are mind controlled to switch to another personality, or personalities, when required for the ritual celebrations. The impact on me as a therapist, and other therapists that I speak to of this sort of information, is initially disbelief, followed by disgust and despair, and then eventually concern for the survivor in the room. But if we consider what we know about the impact of trauma on the development of the self, and the maintenance of the self, or the destruction of the self, we can be overwhelmed by thinking about what must have happened to the individual as a child. It is even more distressing to recognise that for most of these people the primary abuser will have been their parent, often their mother. As a mother myself I cannot understand how anyone can behave that way. But as a therapist I can recognise that the mothers are also victims within the whole process.

What do we do as therapists to keep going? The first thing we do is make sure we have good supervision. The supervision needs to be provided by someone familiar with the issues. It can be difficult to take some of the more bizarre stories to another person, and it is reassuring to discover that the supervisor has heard similar stories before. The Clinic for Dissociative Studies and the European Association, between them, are assembling some bodies of research and information that is helpful. It is enabling more people to have the confidence to work as therapists in this field. More importantly it is making sure that appropriate therapy is available for victims of ritual abuse and mind control programming. Alison Miller has published two quite substantial texts on the subject. In her books she draws heavily on the experience of survivors.

Having found connections with others with experience, the next process for the therapist to consider is their own personal reaction to the material that is being presented to them in therapy. The therapist who finds that they cannot connect with the client and the material clearly cannot provide effective therapy. Assuming that they can recognise mind control programming as a phenomenon, and accept the person sitting there has had that horrendous experience, the next stage is to find their own resilience and tolerance. This is a requirement if weekly or twice-weekly therapy is to be provided and be effective. The therapist needs to be prepared for whatever they are presented with in each session. One of the particular patterns of therapy with a mind control person is that there is no pattern. Each session may bear little relationship to previous sessions, there may be different programmed alters present, there may be mischievous alters present with the role of making the therapist forget what was spoken about in a previous session. Each session will start with an open mind and a willingness to work with whoever and whatever is present. This can be very tiring. It is therefore necessary to make sure that you are well prepared for the session by not being overtired, and not too many clients with mind control are on the caseload at any one time.

## References

Miller A (2012) *Healing the Unimaginable*. Karnac: London.

Miller A (2018) *Becoming Yourself.* Karnac: London.

Sinason V (1992) *Mental handicap and the human condition.* Free Association: London.

# Chapter 12: Training for support staff

Pat Frankish and Carrie Anne Smith

Training support staff on the subject of Dissociative Identity Disorder (DID) and mind programming may seem like a daunting task, however as long as you are honest with your staff about the complexities of the subject you can be surprised just how easily it can become to carry out this task. By using three simple presentations, each getting more in depth than the last, your staff can become versed in enough knowledge about DID and mind control to be able to support their clients in the most effective way possible. Through the use of PowerPoint presentations, with factual slides, points of reflection and direct questions that consolidate the staff members' understanding, along with some interspersed diagrams, it is possible to train a team of supporters with the skills and knowledge that will stand the test of time.

Information that is put across to staff needs to be complex enough to stretch their learning, while at the same time being simple enough to be consumed in small bites. We found that when preparing training, small sections helped staff to take in more information, while consolidation questions where each person was asked how they felt about a particular topic going round the room, helped to put each person in the survivor's shoes, and directly invited people to better understand the subject being broached. It can be a bit daunting having the survivors helping to train the staff, but overall it allows for more honesty among staff and clients, and allows for alters to come forward and shed more light on a particular subject. This helps the training to be more 'real'.

So what works in presentations about DID and mind programming? Here is a breakdown of the training sessions our system took part in.

## Defining the problem

The first issue to tackle was to establish with supporters the Diagnostic Statistical Manual (DSM)-V of mental disorders' definition of DID, as there were staff who had been in the team for some time while others were new to the condition and did not understand it greatly. This laid the foundations to helping people to understand what DID is on the more basic of levels. This was then augmented with an overview of our system, with highlighted points, so people could appreciate how large our system was and how there were subsystems, both light and dark, all of whom operated within our one body. Training needs to have personalised parts to it as well as those of a more generalised nature, otherwise there may not be enough understanding of specific alters within the system that support workers are being trained about, which can lead to confusion.

There then needs to be some generalised explanation as to what Satanic Ritual Abuse actually is, as it incorporates all types of abuse. This also applies to an explanation of mind control/programming. Ritual abuse, it should be noted, contains elements of all types of abuse, but it mostly includes sexual abuse, physical abuse, torture, psychological abuse, emotional abuse, and ritual abuse itself, whereby abuse takes place of all of the above natures within the confines of Satanist, sadistic ideological rituals. Spiritual abuse can also be included.

Where all these types of abuse are included in ritual abuse, mind control is also a regular feature that is contained within it. Mind control is as penetrating as any kind of abuse, in fact more so. Hypnosis, the manipulation of psychological techniques, literal spinning in combination with hypnosis, the use of childhood toys, brain splitting techniques and numerical designation codes of alters, to name but a few, are all combined to manipulate and make a mind-controlled slave who will do the bidding of the mind control programmer, be it self-torture, theft, sexual acts or even suicide. Both personal experiences and more generalised information present a clear picture of ritual abuse, and more importantly, of mind control.

It can then be useful to go round the room and find out what the supporters' preconceptions are about mind control. By finding out what people think it is, you can get an idea of how seriously people take it, which lays the foundations for talking more deeply and completely about what it actually is. It needs to be explained that, through the use of this manipulative technique, mind controllers can make people believe anything and everything they want them to, to the degree that they can actually isolate alters into pre-defined groups so they will do the mind control handler's exact bidding. They can even make alters forget memories of abuse through the direct manipulation of the system's mind. Further information of mind control can also be given at this point. Information such as the fact it usually starts at an early age, involves the use of physical techniques and belief-related and psychological techniques, and involves the use of everyday songs such as nursery rhymes, and children's toys such as spinning tops.

Moving on, it is important to then understand what triggers are, so supporters do not trigger an alters' programming or bad memories. We felt it was important to firstly establish the staff's preconceived ideas of what a trigger actually was, as a talking point to break up all of the information that they were already processing. After going round the room, it was helpful to establish with the support staff a 'working' idea of what triggers are, so they knew what to be careful of in conversation, as well as other ways in which people could be affected. Essentially, a trigger can be something that causes sensory overload and cause memories to come back to the system, programmes to start and much distress and dissociation. Examples of this include – something that is seen, something that is heard, something that is spoken, somatic memories (something felt within the body), tone of voice, certain colours, hand signals and certain places. It can then be useful to point out examples of triggers that are specific to the system the supporters work with. This can greatly assist with helping support workers to get to know their clients better, and in turn get to know what is safe to say and do and what to avoid.

## Getting to know the systems you work with

Having established the basic principles of DID, ritual abuse and mind programming, it is then helpful to start learning more specific details about the DID system that is in question. At this point, we included a session in which staff could shout out names of alters that they had met, which gave them an opportunity to get to know these alters' roles within the system. It also gave the chance for alters to come out in the training session and explain who they were. This then gives a chance to explain why the survivors came about, such as being 'born' as a result of trauma, the fact that some alters came about as a result of hypnosis, and that there are both light and dark alters who all occupy one body.

Explaining to support staff about dark alters that inhabit the body is a useful thing to do next, as it establishes with everyone what to look for when these alters are in the body. We have a number of dark alters in our system, but one group of three that were particularly troublesome were 'the others.' These dark inside people were programmed into the body by our abusers and were based on three people who were particularly evil. Their role within the system was to taunt and maim to a point of internal psychosis, which in turn discredited other alters who wanted, for example, to go to the police. They caused a lot of damage and took up an awful lot of time in therapy, as we struggled to come to terms with the fact that they existed and were not going anywhere. By introducing these dark ones to the supporters, they can be aware of what is happening and how to offer support for our system. This is very advantageous to both staff and clients alike as they are both 'singing from the same hymn sheet', as it were.

Consolidation of this information then took the form of going round the supporters and asking them what example they could give to describe these dark alters, for example a constant radio that you could not switch off, as this helped to establish in the supporter's minds just what these inside people were capable of. Beyond this, it was important to let staff know how the dark ones affected us personally, examples including them threatening to make us paranoid, and them leaving us wondering whom to trust as they whisper about us in the background. This helps supporters to understand the lengths programmers will go to in order to maim and scar their victims.

Finally, it seemed pertinent to explain to staff the established coping mechanisms that work with these dark alters, and that will help the DID system to work through the trials that come as a result of their existence. This included ways of working with us that staff had already found successful, that could be shared with other staff so everyone was working together. These diverse tactics are personal to each system, however it is not pertinent to explain all of our coping mechanisms here. Finally, we asked the staff for ways they could think of that would help us to fight back. This was designed to help them to think of unique coping mechanisms and helped each support worker to work with us individually. Staff's ideas can be tailored to how they work with their clients, which is useful to enhance an individual's working relationships with all of their clients.

The final informative slide focused on the importance of teamwork. This is a foundational and important way of working with any DID system. Without teamwork, a support system may not be successful. It may be useful to also highlight to supporters that it is not their job to carry out therapy, but rather be a supportive aid to the system's psychologist's or therapist's therapy, and just be a listening ear that does not try to 'cure' anything. Confidentiality, too, is a key feature of supporting the clients because trust is very fragile, as is discouraging secrets and lies within the supportive relationship, as this can cause a system to feel scared or triggered. Finally, it is imperative that psychological support is available to support staff teams, be this to educate or to support staff when the therapeutic relationship gets too much to bear. By having this facility, you can have a happy and fulfilled staff team, and a much more peaceful group of clients, even in the hard times, as singing from the same therapeutic hymn sheet and having an agreed way of working is the most important point to strive for.

## Dark alters

The second PowerPoint presentation focused on the deeper aspects of DID and the darker alters in our system. The first objective was to recap on the DID lessons that had already been learnt in the first training session. Speaking about the last time we met allowed supporters to get back into the subject and readied them for what was to come next. Following the recap came information about the way the system had evolved, telling of the way 'the others' in the dark section of our system had taken on new forms of evil, which included the use of hypnotic techniques, which had subsequently caused a fear of controlling people for all of us on the light side. This kind of honesty with support staff is always useful, because it allows them to have an insight into what is going on for the system, and indeed have a more empathetic understanding.

To focus on the subject of fear, our system then wanted people to stand in our shoes, and understand the experiences that people with a history of ritual abuse and mind control actually go through. A talking point was then included – a life lived in fear is not a life – and then they were asked what their thoughts were on this. This allowed staff to expound on what it felt like to live the way they live, and see things from a more expanded point of view. It then gave time for more personal information to be given on the subject of fear and what it meant for us as a system. Fear, for us, was created with examples such as 'the others', putting visualisations of an electric chair in the mind of one of our alters because he was made to do some horrible things by the coven. They also tried to trigger the eating disorder programming within our system by talking constantly about food and weight in a very negative way. This then caused hypervigilance as we struggled to come to terms with the impact of what was happening, which in turn caused panic, depression and suspiciousness amongst us all.

When thinking about what supporters can do to reassure, support and avoid letting paranoia setting in in the DID system you are supporting, there are some simple steps that we found useful that can encourage openness and clarity between supporters and clients. Examples include when the staff phone rings, please do reassure us by saying something like, "This call is not about you, so please don't worry if I have to shut the door during the conversation". During handovers, please know that talking about us in the third person triggers us, so please do not do this. If you do have to have the door shut, please reassure us that you are not speaking ill of us. When scared we are best able to take handovers between staff with the door open. Also, if we are convinced we are being followed by abusers, please reassure us that this is not the case, or take down some details to see if they materialise again. Finally, please respect that switches may occur when we are out, so if we believe people are talking about us, please reassure us and inform us if you did not hear the conversation. We would like to suggest that by using suggestions like these you can encourage a more peaceful atmosphere, which in turns reflects on both the wellbeing of the staff and clients.

It then seemed pertinent to talk about other dark alters within the system apart from 'the others'. This directly challenged staff to remember what they had learnt in the first training session, when dark alters were introduced. Again, we asked staff to call out the names of dark alters within our system. This time we waited to tell the staff the roles of these alters until the next slide. The reason for this was so as to be clear about which of these alters roles were within the system. Satan, The Hypnotiser and The Internal Programmer are just three examples of dark alters within our system. We then went on to explain exactly what they were capable of, so supporters knew what the dangers were of having them around.

In 2017 one of many of our abusers, the father of our body, died. This brought up many feelings for the dark alters inside that were very different to the feelings the rest of us experienced. When an abuser dies, it can bring many conflicting feelings among the system. This however can be helped in many ways – supporting the dark alters to grieve can be healing for them. Allowing dark alters time to process and talk about their emotions is a very useful therapeutic tool. Please be patient, however, if they display anger or hurt, as this can help them process their feelings and can even in some cases allow them to come to the light side. Finally, if you feel unable to support dark alters yourself because you have conflicting feelings, then please contact your system's psychologist or therapist, as they can help you work through your own feelings about what has happened.

To consolidate the knowledge that had been gleaned on dark alters, it was then time for another talking point. We asked two poignant questions of each staff member present at the training.

1. How do you think you would feel if a dark alter was with you in the body now?
2. What would you do to counteract any negative feelings that arose from this encounter?

These questions were designed to really make staff think about what they would do if someone hostile, for example, entered the body. By using these questions, it can be possible for staff to 'brace for impact' and know what to do should this situation arise.

Dark alters are very obviously programmed to behave the way they do, so next it seemed logical to help supporters to understand more about the programming they, and indeed many of us received. We started this section by explaining different types of programming that a system may receive. These included: spin programming, omega or 'end time', programming, sexual beta programming, alpha or general interference programming, Alice in Wonderland experimental (suicide and 'insanity') programming, Wizard of Oz programming, and Greenbaum programming.

It was then time to pause, reflect and then answer the following two questions: how do you feel about mind control programming? Does it scare you? These questions were asked to help staff to understand how they felt about the programming within our system. For many people it is scary to admit that there are people in the world who would literally 'brainwash' a mind control victim in this day and age. These questions were therefore designed to gently assist the supporters to consider how they felt about our programming, and face their fears about working with us, despite this phenomenon.

To help staff face and accept programming was present in our system, we then told them more about what programming actually is. This involved explaining the many techniques and approaches that have been explored in this book; that mind programming is a way of controlling people like us to the extent that they take over their mind and actions, and it's also a way of putting light side alters into roles that appear to make them at fault. By this we mean that, alters can be made to do things that are not of their own choosing, that have consequences of a very negative nature. Programming is next a way of setting triggers in place which activate alters into doing the master programmer's bidding, and finally, it is a way of taking over a person using evil actions, which then allows them to take them over, by the use of controlling behaviours. However scary programming may seem, the Psychic Surgeon in our DID system wanted people to know about hypnosis (see pp.31-33).

Following this explanation, we included some questions about hypnosis in order to gauge how far supporters understood what they had been told. These questions were as follows – what are your feelings about hypnosis? Do you believe in its ability and power to control? How would you feel if you saw one of us in a trance state? Would you panic, or would you be able to calmly execute the actions I have described? By being alert supporters can help our system, and indeed other systems, to come out of trance states and in doing so the therapeutic relationship between staff and clients can be deepened, as it was in our case.

## Controlling behaviour

We then moved on to the use of controlling behaviour, which, as a result of the programming we and other systems have received, can be very emotionally triggering. Telling a system what to do without asking or without prior warning can cause meltdowns due to the different rates that alters work through or process what has been said. The success of telling a system what to do therefore depends on how it is done – because of the way abuse victims have been treated, being too aggressive or forceful does not work and a more gentle approach is more appropriate, as one might expect when dealing with victims of trauma. Next, if a system is dealing with a particularly bad memory, telling them to 'snap out of it' does not work and the system may become angry or paranoid, depending on the memory.

It is also important to be aware that dark alters inside the system can try to fuel controlling behaviour to the maximum effect. If this is the case, it is vital to reassure the system that you are not the alters fuelling the behaviours. These are tried and tested methods of supporting without control that we personally have found to work.

It is important to stress to supporters here that personal reflection on how they, as supporters, would like to be treated if something significant in their own life was changing or if they were being told what to do is really useful. How would they like to be treated in this situation, and what would cause them anger or anxiety? This is a good way to start a conversation about these issues as it allows supporters to understand how their clients would like to be treated without control.

Talk of control, for our system, then focussed on dark alters and how they attempt to control and trigger us. Dark alters can torment systems at any time of the day or night and can be 'sneaky' in their approaches. They can pretend to be light side alters, thus confusing staff and some alters even try to make light-side insiders give false confessions in order to discredit them and lose their supporters. By removing supporters, the system may return to the coven undetected. Dark alters may also make references to sexual experiences, pregnancy and weight, which can directly trigger memories that alters want to forget. This can in turn cause a system to keep secrets from staff, as clients struggle to talk about these subjects because they are 'embarrassing' and/ or triggering. These dark alters within our system have also tried to pretend to be all sorts of people in authority in an attempt to make us look 'mad', thus discrediting everyone within the system. However, by being forewarned you are forearmed and can learn how to counteract their attempts. It is then possible to ask the support staff for their personal ideas on how to counteract dark alters and what they are doing.

There are in fact a number ways of supporting your clients with dark alters that are easier than you think. These include the use of humour – 'having a laugh' over dark alters' antics can strengthen the client's resolve to fight, and, at the end of the day, laughing is much better than crying. Another way of helping the system is to invite other light-side alters to come out and give the host a rest. The host is on the frontline, so some down-time is always welcome. By acknowledging facial expressions and body languages you can learn to gauge switches between alters, both dark and light. This helps you to get to know who is around. If dark alters keep talking at other alters, by asking what they are saying, you too can also take a weight off the host's shoulders, as this helps remind clients that dark alters' beliefs that they are in authority is a silly assumption and can help them start to lose their power. It can also be useful to know that, if all else fails, you can ask for a protector within your DID system to come out and help bring the host back if they are struggling.

As a system, we do not have a lot of confidence in our abilities, and since the subject of mind control and triggers is such a serious subject, it seemed important to finish with some humour. This we did by asking the supporters how they would describe the dark alters in a funny way. This can bring many laughs, and brings the whole team and clients together for any questions that need to be asked.

## Stone alters

Another type of alter whom you may encounter in supporting your DID system is the 'stone' alters. 'Stone' alters for us took the form of highly hypnotised alters who were a by-product of re-programming . These alters also may have had psychic surgery performed upon them. This form of 'surgery', may take the form of hypnotically removing the use of certain parts of the body, and did for our system. 'Stone' people talk sleepily and cannot move their body much, if at all, and may come and go, depending on the pull on them to resurface. It is therefore vital to encourage stone people to fight their stoniness. If they do not fight, they may never be able to heal and learn to live a meaningful life.

Stone people in a DID system, need some very specific qualities that can be found in their support. Again, there is a need for all support staff to sing off the same hymn sheet as it were. This is because consistency in support is the only way in which stone people can heal and live life to the full. There also needs to be a gentle firmness amongst supporters, and an ability to keep stone alters centred on the voices of staff rather than those inside who seek to pull them back into the hypnotic state that they were in before. Stone inside people need to keep doing activities of daily living as well, because there needs to be some sense of normality in the lives of these people where everything is hypnotic. Washing, cooking and showering are all examples of activities that can help to bring a sense of normality to these alters' lives. The alters in this stage of recovery are in an acute stage of healing, so if you can lift them out of their trance state, you will play a big part in them gaining a meaningful life. (Please note that hypnosis is different from fatigue and tiredness and it is important not to be confused by them.)

To bring people who are stone out of trance states needs special techniques – simply clapping in someone's face to snap them out of it will only serve to shock and retraumatise the system concerned. There a number of techniques which can be employed to bring stone people out of their hypnotic state. Firstly, you can ask them to open their eyes if they are closed. This can help the stone people to start to become reaccustomed to the here and now, instead of being inside their hypnotic state. Once the inside person concerned has their eyes opened, you can ask them to notice their surroundings. This can include the colour of the walls in the room, or the pattern of the curtains at the windows; anything around them at all that will assist them in grounding themselves.

You can also ask them to notice sensory objects around them. Feeling the texture of the sofa, or a cuddly toy or cushion rubbed against the inside person's face, can all stimulate the brain out of a post-hypnotic trance state. If by this time the alter concerned is sufficiently lucid to be able to move, then ask them to move in the space they are in. Even if this means moving their arms, or moving their torso forward, all of these movements are helping to reacclimatise the inside stone person into the here and now. Another technique that can be used to bring someone back is to try the 7/11 breathing technique. This involves asking the client to breathe in for a count of seven seconds, and then breathe out for a count of 11. This can assist to stop any hyperventilation that may be going on as a result of coming out of hypnosis, if this is abrupt in manner, but also causes the inside person to focus in on their breathing, which in turn can bring them back into their own body, and not into a post-hypnotic trance state. Finally, if all of these techniques fail to work, it can be useful to count the person out of the hypnotic state. This can be done by counting backwards, from five to one, with accompanying references to being more and more awake, as described in the previous presentation.

## Understanding how mind programming works

The final presentation was entitled 'Tears are a silent scream', which refers to something one of our male alters said – "Tears (and indeed emotional pain) are a scream that never escapes the mouth". This phrase to us epitomises mind control. The scream is never allowed to escape the mouth because of the nature of brainwashing.

Taking the example of a robot whose function is to build cars, we reintroduced the idea of programming to the support staff. A robot is inputted with information to control and fulfil its task. It is inputted to do its task and nothing more. This is like the lives of a programmed DID system. Life for them is more of an existence than a meaningful life, with no emotions, fun or meaning, rather it just being a myriad of nothingness. In essence it is like telling a person they are a giant panda and them blindly believing it is the truth. However, the person believing this statement can then be asked, "Just because I call you a giant panda, does this make you one?" This directly challenges the person to think outside of what they were told.

Trying to break a long life of programming is a very hard thing to do. So we then introduced humour into the presentation again, by asking the supporters "To what extent is programming like turkeys voting for Christmas?" We also asked "How can this type of unawareness of control hamper innocent lives in this situation?" This question about turkeys and Christmas can be likened to a programmed system blindly living without the majority of the system knowing that they have suicide programming inside and going on without knowing it is there. This is what hampers innocent lives, and can literally lead to a life and death situation.

Moving on from this scenario, we then felt it important to explain what programming is, and indeed what it is not. We explained that firstly and most importantly it is a method of controlling a system's lives by the use of hypnosis, psychological techniques and triggers, to name but a few examples, as explored in previous chapters of this book. It is also a way of hiding alters within the system, so no one knows they are there. It can be a method of making a system want to harm or kill their own body through the use of 'omega' or 'end-time' programming. Another way programming can affect people is to isolate those subjected to it. Ways of describing what programming is not is to start by explaining that it is not simply attention-seeking behaviour, such as attempted self/selves injury. It is also not to be feared, as talking about mind control can be the key to unravelling it. Finally, it is useful to explain to supporters that their clients cannot just 'snap out' of a programming flare up. Like any physical illness it can take time to go back into the fulness of 'remission'.

## Spotting the signs of programming

It is also useful to verse supporters in some basic information about what to look for should these types of mind control become active. Apart from knowing about the types of programming (see pp.23-24) it is also imperative that supporters know the tell-tale signs that mind control, 'brainwashing', is active. A good starting point here is to ask a question that is personal to the system being supported. In our case this was "Are there any tell-tale signs which are evident in us that you think are from the programming? Please pay special attention to alpha and omega or 'end-time' programming."

There are physical signs of end-time (omega) programming and spin programming which supporters need to take note of, in case they are in evidence with the system they are working with. Scratching, biting and digging nails into the systems skin, just to cause pain and instances of deliberately and constantly picking at it, can all be signs that Omega programming is active. Stockpiling and hoarding medication, and doing this by not taking needed medication, are also signs that this type of programming is getting to a critical stage. Alters may hide knives and other sharps for use later as part of this lethal programming, or they may even burn or cut the body, or perform other types of dangerous self-injury, such as trying to drink cleaning products. Trichotillomania (alters pulling out their own hair) can be another sign that alters' stress levels due to active programming are high. If you see an alter tapping up their veins, or indeed planning where cuts are going to happen, then this is another sign of end-time programming, as is stabbing at their fingers, for example with a fork. Finally, alters putting their affairs in order, as mentioned earlier in this chapter, is a pretty sure sign that omega is in a dangerous stage. This list is not limited to just these actions, but anything that makes a staff member suspicious of programming phenomena, should be reported to the leader of your system's service.

Spin programming is another complex form of programming that you may see exhibited in the system you are working with. Spin programming combines, for the most part, literal physical upside-down spinning, combined with hypnosis and other terror filled experiences when it is taking place. For us this took place by being spun upside down from the garage roof, to make us dizzy and submissive to whatever the head programmer said. Signs of spin programming include making circular movements with the body in a specific direction, which for us was clockwise. We also appeared to anyone watching, to be in a hypnotic state as explored in the last presentation. Alters are compelled and are therefore unable to stop the circular movements they are making, which can come from being taught to spin like a spinning top when the body was at a very young age. Finally, all alters within the system being supported may feel the same way about a programmed element for example suicide, when spin programming is active. These are classic signs of spin programming and as such, should be taken notice of should they happen.

We next asked support staff how they could help us to stop the programming as this gave them some useful steps to take in difficult situations. We also asked them if there was anything practical they felt they could do to help us. This was a useful talking point as the ideas they had were very often different to our own. The ways we have found that staff can be useful include talking to us and reassuring us, even if it is just about everyday things, and using diversionary tactics, especially those requiring a degree of concentration such as playing board games and crafts. (However please keep items that are dangerous to the system in a locked cupboard or staff-only room that the DID system cannot go in without their agreement.) Another way of helping is to encourage us not to bite or pick skin, or pull out hair etc. This decreases the likelihood of the clients selves-harming. If you are also aware of an alter tapping up veins please ask the inside person concerned not to carry out their plan. The other alternative is to ask for a protector alter to come through and stop the behaviours happening. If an alter is spinning in this state, then please ask them to spin in the opposite direction, as it can stop the spinning in its tracks. If this does not work, or you are concerned that something is not OK, then please contact the lead psychologist or therapist for further assistance. They can allay your fears and assist you further.

## Alpha programming

Firstly, it is useful to consider the role of alpha programming in a DID system. Alpha programming is known as 'general interference' programming and involves interfering in any way in which the programmer can with the victim's thinking and functioning. It can also involve the use of cued phrases or words that trigger a victim to avoid subjects or forget things, thus confusing incidents and traumas so a victim cannot tell their truths, and involves the use of anything that can stop the victims from thinking coherently. Alpha programming is primarily a way of stopping the victims functioning coherently and is the 'first-line' attack in Dr Greenbaum's programming structure.

So how do you help to block Alpha programming? Talking to a system about anything in the light and keeping us talking despite what is going on helps. It Is also useful to learn to recognise cue words and triggers as this can help to stop the programming in its tracks. In light of this, it is important to remember that if you come across a trigger or cue-word you must pass them onto the service-lead and each other as forewarned is forearmed! Finally, please do allow an alter to talk if they are struggling to function, as together we may be able to put together part of the programming 'jigsaw'.

It is helpful to check in with support staff how they feel about working with cues and triggers and whether or not staff feel that their clients can heal from Alpha programming. It is important for all supporters to know that whilst complete healing from Greenbaum programming may not be possible, it is more than appropriate to say that a degree of healing and a meaningful life can be achieved with support. Without the hope of a meaningful life, hope is gone, and that is a very daunting place to be.

Another type of Greenbaum programming that supporters need to know about is Omega or 'End time', programming.This form is characterised firstly, by alters wanting to kill their body, but not necessarily having an inclination as to why. It may also literally be the only option to the alters concerned, and all they have been trained to do. This is so finely honed, that alters with suicide programming switches only know how to do this at all costs, without further conversation on the subject. If spin programming is working in conjunction and has been spun through the programme and the system as a whole, then all alters within it may become suicidal. This is because when information is spun through a system, all alters have no choice but to go with it due to their programming. To symbolise the ending of the alters lives, there may be signs such as ending attachments, giving up previously enjoyed activities, or getting rid of property. For us, it has literally been a case of putting our lives in order in preparation for suicide.

## Supporting the supporters

At this point it was important to check in with how support staff felt about what they had learnt so far, and so we asked two questions as a talking point:

1. How does the thought of the details on programming that we have told you so far make you feel?
2. Are you feeling overwhelmed, or does it intrigue and interest you, in terms of how you can help?

By asking these questions we were checking that staff were not scared or phased by what they had learnt, as this was not conducive to working with our system. It is important that staff believe in programming otherwise non-belief can potentially cause ruptures in a support staff team, and indeed can cause further trauma for the survivors being supported.

Support staff need support too, to be able to support us, and so we next looked into how to support them in working with us. By doing these simple steps it is possible to bring greater equilibrium to the therapeutic relationships between staff and clients. In the middle of all the programming talk, it is important for all staff to take gentle care of themselves even in the more difficult situations. If you don't understand what is going on for the system being supported, then you can always ask us. Never be afraid to ask questions: they are a way of understanding more about what is going on for the system. Remember too not to take your worries and problems from work home with you, as this can cause you psychological damage if you are not careful. Please remember that 'this too shall pass'. By this we mean that everything will subside eventually, given time. Also, remember that we are receiving psychological support so you do not need take responsibility for all of our trauma. Finally, please remember to access support from the psychologist/therapist at the head of your service if you are struggling with anything or have any concerns. By doing this you can find working in this environment a lot easier to cope with.

Finally it seemed of great importance to ask supporters how they felt about having programming knowledge at their fingertips. We needed to know if this knowledge empowered support staff, or indeed if it scared them, in which case further training may be needed. We felt that knowledge is key to empowering staff to work in more effective ways with us, as it potentially takes the fear out of working with this challenging subject. Also, teaching people about programming can assist in taking the complexity out of the situation in which support staff may find themselves.

Teaching support staff about the DID system they are working with, their triggers, conditions, limited abuse history and programming is crucial (with the system's consent) as it enables supporters to more effectively work with their clients and maximise the therapeutic relationships they have with them. Honesty is the best policy, and however scary it is for the system concerned, techniques can be learnt by both supporters and the DID system that will make life more meaningful, but also it allows both parties to acknowledge the depth of trauma the system has gone through. And while this will not take the abuse and mind control programming away, it can go a long way to helping every person within the system to live a more fulfilled life.

This training can now be purchased from Frankish Training.

# Section 4: Conclusion

This section summarises what is possible and necessary to support the victims of mind programming, and what offers real hope for the future.

# Chapter 13: How much is understood by professional services?

Pat Frankish

I have been involved with people with Dissociative Identity Disorder (DID), like Carrie Anne, for many years. Valerie Sinason was the first person to share her knowledge and, although we have followed slightly different paths, we have continued to work together and support each other. A major part of our pioneering work has been the education of others, and the establishment of a knowledge base that enables service commissioners to make the right decisions. Decisions that lead to safety and recovery by providing the right things at the right time.

There are several different strands to this, which I will discuss in this chapter. One, obviously, is building awareness through research and publications, of which this book is a part. The second is the establishment of National Institute for Health and Care Excellence (NICE) guidelines; something that is still in progress. The third is individual therapy for those who can manage with out-patient support, and the fourth is the provision of 24-hour support for the more extreme and risk-prone people/systems.

The research side of this is difficult. The ethical position is complicated: how can a divided/complex 'self' give consent to be part of a study? They can't. So we are left with practice-based evidence, growing the body of knowledge from experience of working with more people. The recognition of the condition of DID as a Post Traumatic Stress Disorder (PTSD) rather than a personality disorder is progress, but we are still a long way from recognising the signs in children. There are no NICE guidelines for detecting dissociation in children, nor are there any for appropriate treatment of adults. Most of the published work has been referred to in this book and by its nature it all falls in the category of soft data. Hard data could be gathered but it would take a large study following a cohort from birth, like a whole town study, and this type of research is time-consuming and expensive. In the meantime, the retrospective data must be used and bringing it together is a study worth doing.

NICE guidelines could be drawn up from existing knowledge, however the main source of data is the Clinic for Dissociative Studies (CDS), founded by Valerie Sinason, and as a charity it is outside of the statutory services. It would seem that only data gathered in the NHS is used in the development of guidelines, and whilst it may be that charitable and independent providers could submit evidence most will not have the financial or personnel resources to be able to do this. The numbers are small, but the distress and danger is huge, and the abused children should be identified in early childhood and rescued. There is a general ignorance and disbelief amongst doctors, other professional staff and the general public, which makes it harder to see.

The third element, individual therapy, has made considerable progress. CDS has become recognised by Clinical Commissioning Groups (CCGs), which are statutory NHS bodies responsible for the planning and commissioning of health care services for their local area. This means that individuals can now access therapy that is funded by their home area using the exceptional referral system, and this has made a huge difference to a lot of people. Therapy, supervision and sometimes a support worker, are funded after an assessment has identified the issue. There are diagnostic assessments that help to define the need. Unfortunately, most CCGs will only have one or two people so they can't justify setting up the whole service themselves, but those authorities that recognise their own lack of resource and expertise are helpful. They are the enlightened ones and they are providing much-needed help. Therapy can be needed for many years for some people. One of the positive consequences of this investment has been seeing people become valuable members of the workforce, often in the same field, and to be able to live a relatively ordinary life.

Holistic, whole-life support is rare: I only know of two people who have this provided as a specialist service, one of whom is Carrie Anne. The other is supported by CDS and a CCG in another part of the country. Both received their support and understanding partly by chance, but primarily by being supported by someone who understood the condition, the need, and the possibility of progress to a better life.

We cannot know how many people with a similar life story have taken their own lives; are still trapped in their living hell; or have been diagnosed as severely mentally ill and detained in long-term hospital placements. We do know it doesn't have to be this way. And yet many CCGs still don't recognise the condition or the need. Current health care checklists don't contain anything that would identify the presence of dissociation and pathways in children and adolescent mental health services (CAMHS) and adult mental health services don't include dissociation. Few mental health practitioners will meet anyone with the condition or know what questions to ask.

There is, therefore, a desperate need for more knowledge to be available. Some training for support staff is available from Frankish Training and described in this book. This is a starting point for a huge staff group to take on a full support package, but there are clear barriers. For a start, they don't know what they don't know. Many people are also disbelieving or afraid of organised abuse. We know there are human traffickers active in the world today, and they will likely be using mind programming to enable them to control their victims. Many of these victims will die or become so ill they are incoherent. Some will become perpetrators themselves. There must be recognition of the condition and the prospect of healing.

It is hoped that this text will help in the future planning of appropriate responses to the horror of organised abuse and the condition of DID which is, in itself, a survival response. The people/systems who survive deserve to be properly supported and cared for.

# Chapter 14: Facing the future: how services can evolve

Pat Frankish

It should have become clear from what you have read so far that supporting somebody with Dissociative Identity Disorder (DID) and mind programming is not simple. As a consequence, most of the individuals responsible for providing support for such people will struggle to know what to do. Over the past 20 years there has been a significant improvement in the range of services provided for individuals with DID across the UK. The Clinic for Dissociative Studies, led by Dr Valerie Sinason, has led the way in helping commissioning authorities to provide the right response at the right time. The link with the European Association has also strengthened the knowledge base on which decisions are made.

Most of the progress that has been made has been in the provision of individual therapy for people with DID and mind control. These usually take the form of twice a week therapy with 90-minute sessions, to allow for the complexity and depth of material to be acknowledged and analysed. Some clinical commissioning groups have now grasped the need for this and will fund it on the basis of a comprehensive assessment by the clinic. Therapy for complex people with multiple selves and mind control is not straightforward and comprehensive supervision also has to be provided. For some people there is an additional need for a support worker to be there to assist with day-to-day challenges and the fallout from therapy. Then there are the even more complex people who need 24-hour support because of their high risk of taking their own lives, or being pulled back to the ritual abuse group that they've escaped from (the experience of the survivor telling her story here).

Helping commissioners to understand the processes involved has proven to be quite difficult. This seems to be, to some extent, because of how hard it is to understand and accept such vile practices as mind control are still happening in modern society. And I think most of us, who work in the services, understand how hard it is to accept. We have all been in that situation ourselves when first encountering our first client. And then it gradually begins to make sense, when we recognise the complexity and severity of the situation. Most people have heard of secret societies although most of us think of them as being works of fiction. And most of us wish that was all they were. But we know that is not the case. People are capable of doing horrendous things to other people. And one of the things that we do recognise, in contact with these organisations, is that there is a generational commitment. So each generation is training the next generation to maintain the organisation. This is no different from lots of ordinary everyday societies and organisations which have their own future proofing, always planning to maintain themselves over long periods of time. This brings into question the need to establish an understanding that can be used without having to go back to the drawing board with each new referral. In the UK, it is usual for an intervention to be scrutinised and established in the NICE guidelines. For a treatment to meet the criteria for acceptance in the guidelines a lot of work is required. There is also a need to establish a firm research base, which in itself means that a large number of people must be studied. The Clinic for Dissociative Studies is accumulating a significant body of information about outpatient treatments and these will hopefully become the basis of new NICE guidelines in the not-too-distant future. It is more complex when we consider people who need 24-hour support.

Following on from what has already been said in this book, it seems that the better approach may be to link the 24 hours support required by people with DID and mind control to the individuals who require trauma informed care. There is no doubt that the condition of DID is a response to trauma. It reflects a survival response to trauma. It follows that the intervention that needs to be provided and purchased must fit with the model of trauma informed care. This model has been described elsewhere in our book Holistic Treatment of People with DID and is summarised here. There are four key elements to trauma informed care. The first is of course the recognition that it is trauma that we're dealing with and that this requires a support response. The first element is that support is provided over a 24-hour period. The second requirement is that the support staff are trained to provide support in the right way for the individual concerned. The third element is that those staff, once trained, are provided with support in the work that they are doing, in recognition of how stressful it can be. And the fourth element is individual therapy for the person with DID to enable them to live as good a life as they can with the condition. As mentioned elsewhere in this book, some people will seek some integration of multiple selves, whereas others will seek synchrony and tolerance.

Helping the individuals who are responsible for commissioning such services is proving to be quite difficult. It is reassuring to know that there are not thousands of people needing this approach. However those that do really do need it, so it is important that we find a way to help the relevant authorities to both understand, accept, and proceed appropriately with their decision-making. It is hoped that this text will help and that more people will become aware of what is needed. Not all people with dissociative identity disorder experience mind control. It may be that the people who have, have more in common with military survivors of torture than of other people we meet in mental health services. Whichever way we look at it, we are looking at trauma and survival. It seems at least likely that quite a few people do not survive long enough to come into treatment. They either take their own lives or are removed by their initial trainers. It is a black and alarming area of life to consider, and most social workers and health professionals will have had no contact with anything like it in their training or their professional lives. Which makes it even more important that notice is taken of the ones who are able to speak out.

As we have brought this book together, with the support and encouragement of Valerie Sinason, Carrie Anne and I have sought to provide an understanding of what we are dealing with, and how we can help. Dr Sinason has worked with this client group for many years and is an internationally recognised expert in the field. Carrie Anne Smith has a lifetime knowledge of the issues and has been brave enough to describe them in her chapters. I have worked hard to draw attention to trauma informed care across client groups over many years and have adapted the approach for anyone who has suffered trauma.

What we would like the authorities to understand is that there is a prospect of progress and an ordinary life. It doesn't have to involve multiple admissions to hospital, multiple self-harm, crisis intervention after crisis intervention and potential suicide. With the right level of support the individual can go on to lead a useful life, accessing their intellect and ability to give something back to society. It seems appropriate that that should be provided.

It may be worth considering slightly different approaches, depending on the severity of the condition in an individual. For some people with DID the availability of individual outpatient therapy may be sufficient to enable them to live a relatively ordinary life. This therapy will usually be for two sessions a week, probably 90 minutes each, and may be for a very long time. It would not be unreasonable to expect to provide supportive psychotherapy for life, in order to meet the need for a reliable attachment figure, without needing a 24-hour presence. There are some support packages provided by the Clinic for Dissociative Studies that include this level of therapy, and may provide a support worker for a few hours a week as well.

There will be some people with dissociative identity disorder and mind control who have benefited from extensive therapy and are able to manage their lives in the mutually acceptable way. They may be able to work, to enter into relationships, and live a relatively ordinary life. It does seem, however, that this is quite difficult for people who have been severely indoctrinated into a ritual abuse group.

The most distressed people, who struggle to hold onto a core self for any length of time, will need 24-hour support, usually in their own single person service. Experience would indicate that they are not safe in a shared residential facility, as the negative alters subvert the system to take the individual into danger. Providing an appropriate single person service stops the repeated admissions to hospital, potential suicide attempts, and the involvement of lots of agencies in trying to sort out crisis after crisis.

# Afterword

Written by one of Carrie Anne Smith's alters, describing their journey and their hopes for the future.

> We have learnt about mind control, living with it and its consequences, and we have learnt about the damage that it does. We have also learnt how there is a need for health and police professionals to learn about mind control and understand the damaging effects that happen as a result of a DID system going through programming, so they know how to understand if a system presents themselves to them, so it is pertinent to consider a very important question – following survival, can a DID system with mind control features have a meaningful life?
>
> The answer to this question is yes! There is a future and the opportunity for a meaningful life. It is evident in the lives of so many survivors of this kind of treatment and we as a system can bear this out.
>
> Although we are still in therapy and need psychological support, we are gradually learning that we can live a meaningful life, that is making a difference to other people, and in turn to ourselves. We are working as a skills teacher with people with a range of disabilities. You cannot take away the pain that the abuse has left us with but, with support we have begun to work with people with varying disabilities just like ourselves, and to teach them a number of different subjects, and all because people have seen that we as a system do have a future. At this point, we must pay tribute to Amanda Brock and Dr Pat Frankish, who saw that we could make a difference, however without the many talents and abilities that our alters have between them, we would not be able to. So it is their bravery and tenacity in a bedlam of hell that have come to the fore, and have proved that we have a future and that we have so much to give!
>
> When I say this, it is not without pain; I cannot stress enough the abreactions and terror that we have gone through to get where we are today. However, although these features of our lives are beginning to lessen a little, the marks of trauma and mind control still remain. As a result of the pain and trauma that we received, we now live with two conditions – Fibromyalgia and Functional Neurological Disorder. We have been told by our neurologist that these illnesses go hand in hand with trauma and require therapy to get them under control, but with the input and support we have, we are gradually learning to work on these two burdens. With the correct combination of therapy and medication along with the support of friends who are so important on this journey of healing, we are able to do our job, and prove to ourselves that we are not the piece of dirt and rubbish that the abusers always used to say that we were. This is a priceless gift

which, although it comes at a high emotional cost, has brought so much joy to our system that you would not believe some of the changes that we see in some of ourselves – even we did not see those at first!

The illnesses we have do impact on our job at times, but we are grateful and indebted to Kelly Calpin for her continuous support along with her team of staff that still support us on a daily basis, who keep us safe and work with us so diligently, to help us be the best that we can be in our new role. They have accepted us as a staff member, and assist us in taking things day by day. They are a blessing to us, and without them being there, we would not be where we are today.

We hear the reader wondering how we have accomplished finding a future... The answer to this is that to be accepted by one person and take their hand and let them take the lead, and just be accepted for all their selves, is like gold dust, but is more than achievable. We never thought that we could or would ever find this, but we did, and that is a gift that money can't buy, so grasp it tight with both hands, and in doing so you too can learn to heal.

We know that it will not be an easy road, but in time we believe that we may be able to go to the legal authorities and report the atrocities done to us, as though there may not be many, there are still sympathetic officers out there who have been trained in DID and mind control. This will happen when our system feels ready, but for now we know we are safe, and that when we are ready we have people who will support us in taking this huge step. The mistakes that we have made in the past, of going before we were ready, mean that we have learnt the hard way that we must  wait until the time is right. But if that means that in time people will be stopped from doing the heinous acts that all but destroyed our lives, then it will be time well spent.

Belief and trust are key to all our truths since leaving the coven, along with a strict no secrets and lies policy, and this has been the key to our moving on to the extent we have. But, overall, I can tell you one truth that you should not forget – there is a future!

I wish you all of the healing that you deserve, and that you will find a peace that transcends all of the hell you went through – and may you find your truths heard so you know that there is a meaningful future there for you – reach out and grab it!

Lioness Kayleigh